TALES OF ST. FRANCIS

Tales
of
St. Francis

MURRAY BODO, O.F.M.

St.
Anthony
MESSENGER
PRESS

CINCINNATI, OHIO

Cover woodcut by David Frampton

Cover by Margot Asahina

ISBN 0-86716-195-7

©1988 by Murray Bodo

Published by arrangement with Doubleday, a division of Bantam Doubleday
   Dell Publishing Group, Inc.

Paperback edition copyright ©1992 by Murray Bodo

Published by St. Anthony Messenger Press

For my mother,
who read me my first stories

CONTENTS

STORY-SPIRITUALITY: AN INTRODUCTION 11

A CHILDHOOD FRIEND 21

THE KNIGHT WHO INSPIRED ST. FRANCIS 24

ST. FRANCIS MEETS A LEPER 26

FATHER AND SON 29

THE POOR PRIEST OF SAN DAMIANO 33

OF BERNARD OF QUINTAVALLE, ST. FRANCIS' FIRST

   COMPANION 36

THE PRIEST WHO BECAME BROTHER SYLVESTER 41

THE POOR WOMAN WHO LIVED IN THE DESERT 45

THE ANGEL OF POGGIO BUSTONE 47

THE HUNGRY BROTHER AND RIVO TORTO 52

THE BENEDICTINES OFFER FRANCIS A CHURCH 55

LADY CLARE OF ASSISI 57

THE WOLF OF GUBBIO 61

ST. DOMINIC AND THE CHAPTER OF MATS 64

THE MISERABLE LEPER'S TALE 67

BROTHER MASSEO'S TALE 70

OF THE PORTIUNCULA INDULGENCE 74

ST. FRANCIS AND THE SULTAN 77

CONTENTS

THE DAMIETTA PROSTITUTE 81

ST. FRANCIS AND BROTHER LEO TRY TO PRAY 84

ON DISCERNING GOD'S WILL 87

BROTHER JUNIPER AND BROTHER JOHN THE SIMPLE 90

BROTHER JUNIPER AND THE FARMER'S PIG 94

HOW BROTHER JUNIPER SEESAWED WITH CHILDREN 100

HOW BROTHER RUFINO PREACHED 102

HOW BROTHER STEPHEN WAS CURED 106

HOW SATAN DECEIVED BROTHER RUFINO 107

BROTHER BERNARD AND THE ANGEL 111

BROTHER ELIAS AND THE ANGEL 113

BROTHER BONIZZO, WITNESS TO THE RULE OF LIFE 116

THE VERSE KING 117

THE BROTHER WHO WANTED TO BE A SOLITARY PILGRIM 120

ANOTHER TALE OF BROTHER PACIFICO 122

OF GRECCIO AND THE FIRST CHRISTMAS CRIB 125

OF PERFECT JOY 128

WINGS 133

A LETTER TO BROTHER LEO 136

ST. FRANCIS SINGS HIS SWAN SONG 141

A SONG FOR THE POOR LADIES 144

THE PHYSICIAN'S TALE 146

CONTENTS

ST. FRANCIS AND THE CELESTIAL ZITHER   149

ST. FRANCIS, THE SOLAR HERO   151

A FRANCISCAN MANTLE   153

ANOTHER TALE OF BROTHER ELIAS   156

TRANSITUS   158

ST. FRANCIS DICTATES HIS TESTAMENT   160

A NUN'S TALE   166

THE GOLDEN SAYINGS OF BROTHER GILES   168

THE ROBBER'S TALE   172

AFTERWORD   179

A CHRONOLOGY OF THE LIFE OF ST. FRANCIS   183

ACKNOWLEDGMENTS   189

STORY-SPIRITUALITY:
AN INTRODUCTION

The tale is not beautiful if nothing
is added to it.

—Tuscan Proverb

The following pages are the result of my own fascination
with stories. My very first memories are intertwined with
stories I heard over and over again as a boy. Stories of
hunting trips in the Rockies, stories of labor meetings in
the coal fields of southern Colorado, stories of Depression
days and mine closings and scabs being shot and how the
tram broke periodically, scattering bodies all over the ragged side of the mountain that fronted our little cabin-house
in Silverton, Colorado. And it was through story that I
first came to know St. Francis, in books like Felix Tim-
mermans' *The Perfect Joy of St. Francis*, G. K. Chesterton's
St. Francis of Assisi, and Paul Sabatier's *Life of St. Francis*.

As I grew older and began to study more seriously the
thirteenth- and fourteenth-century stories of St. Francis
and his early companions I fell under their spell, their
charm and folklike quality, their multiplicity of styles and
viewpoints; and I began to wonder what would be revealed
in retelling the stories that have shaped and formed my
own life as a twentieth-century Franciscan.

And so I began this book, a work of joy, to be sure, yet
something more. I noticed very early on that something
beyond delight was happening inside me. Each story was a

further exploration of my own spiritual roots, a stronger bonding with my Franciscan brothers and sisters, past and present. And my own voice began to change as I realized that in retelling these stories, I was somehow realigning myself with what I dearly love. The storytelling became an act of humility before my spiritual ancestors, and the resultant connectedness, the communion with them that I began to experience, became the underlying justification for this book.

This principle of integration in turn became the principle of selection: I began to choose only those stories that have that mysterious, archetypal quality that speaks to something profound within us, some deep desire of the human heart.

That strong pull upon the heart is what kept me working on these stories; and as I continued to let them tell themselves, a whole spirituality began to emerge as people and places and happenings started coming together into a vibrant picture of Gospel living. Rather than becoming a method of arriving at Christian maturity, these stories became for me the journey itself. Like prayer, they took me along with them and somehow effected in me inner transformations not unlike those experienced by Francis and his companions. And that, no doubt, is what story-spirituality is all about.

Whoever told the first stories was not only remembering, but reliving, as well. And what he or she remembered was conditioned by what had happened within, those unforgettable changes in attitude and behavior that reveal the Spirit's presence in our lives. The stories, then, are the incarna-

tion of the efficacy of God's Word. They flesh out the idea
that God's Word does not return to God empty, and their
very retelling itself becomes an effective word, moving the
reader to action within and without.

Sometimes the early Franciscan stories become overly di-
dactic and preachy and try too hard to make a point. I
noticed that those stories seldom did anything to me or for
me. But when the story was simply story—spontaneous,
unself-conscious of any apologetic or proselytizing purpose
—then the genuineness of the story would authenticate the
experience it was narrating.

When the story witnessed to the actual experiences of St.
Francis and his companions, it drew me into it and moved
me to want to live a more genuine Christian life. But when
the story was really a disguised attempt to *make* me try to
live a more perfect life, the story would cease to be story,
and I could not enter into it and travel with the characters.
I've excluded most of those stories here, and some might
see in that decision a prejudice and manipulation not unlike that of the storyteller whose story I've excluded. But
that, too, is part of story-spirituality: we retell what is true
to our own experience; we retell those stories that, when
we read them, make us feel that someone finally under-
stands us and sees life the way we see it.

Storytelling, like hearing or reading a story, is selective.
It is our own experience that continues to accept or reject
the genuineness of experiences other than our own. My
main rationale, then, for what I have included or excluded
of the early stories is whether or not they rang true for me,

whether or not I was moved by what happened in their retelling. When I had doubts, I would look to see if the story was repeated by other early writers and how it was told. If the story was consistently retold, I included it in spite of my own skepticism, believing that something in me was refusing the challenge of the story. A good story not only affirms us and confirms our experience; it also challenges and expands us.

In the end, however, it is the stories we like that we retell. I have been reading and delighting in the stories of St. Francis and his companions for over thirty-five years, and these are the ones I like best and that have played a large part in my understanding of what it means to be a Christian and a Franciscan.

The early stories of St. Francis are a special kind of story —not accurate in the sense that a chronicle or objective account is accurate, but accurate in recapturing a Spirit-filled time. They convey what it was like for St. Francis and his companions to live in the Spirit. And they are written down by those who either experienced that life themselves or longed to rekindle that original fervor in their own time. And so these stories are real, true, only when read with spiritual eyes. Without those eyes, they seem mere fantasies, legends fabricated by the imagination. The stories of St. Francis and his companions demand of the reader the faith of those who lived them, the faith of those who recorded them.

These stories, then, are accounts not simply of the lives

of the first Franciscans but of those happenings in their lives which moved them to faith, a joy-filled faith that comes from taking what is bitter in life and embracing it for the love of Jesus Christ, who in turn transforms it into sweetness of soul.

In addition, when they tell *what* happened to the early Franciscans, the stories end up telling us *why* as well. So that, taken together, the stories provide an account not only of the joy of Francis and his companions but of the cause of that joy.

And that is the source of the wisdom they impart; that is why we continue to read them. They satisfy our longing for something beyond. They tell us that from time to time we see the eternal in its workings upon people who have entered into that other world of the Spirit. They show us people who have made the passage beyond and how that happens. Sometimes the passage is recounted as wholly the work of God; at other times it is pictured as happening when people live their lives in such a way that God makes the kingdom of heaven appear for them again, as in the days of the Apostles.

For example, St. Francis and his companions start living the First Beatitude of Jesus in earnest, and their life together starts looking like the kingdom of God on earth, thus fulfilling Jesus' words, "How blessed are the poor in spirit, the kingdom of heaven is theirs" (Mt 5:3). Jesus does not say, "The kingdom of heaven *will be* theirs," but "The kingdom of heaven *is* theirs," here and now. And that is what Francis and his companions experienced and what the stories recount: if you live in poverty of spirit, wonders begin to happen among you, and true joy as well, for the kingdom of God is indeed here.

But the stories do not restrict themselves to the First Beatitude. There are other sayings the early Franciscans live by, such as "Set your heart on his kingdom first, and on God's saving justice, and all these other things will be given you as well" (Mt 6:33). And "If you wish to be perfect, go and sell your possessions and give the money to the poor, and you will have treasure in heaven; then come, follow me" (Mt 19:21). And on and on, until we begin to see that living in and for the kingdom involves embracing all the words of God and, ultimately, the Incarnate Word of God, Jesus himself. Living in the Word made flesh and then enfleshing God's words in one's own life seems mere fantasy and illusion to those without the eyes of faith. And seeing with the eyes of faith begins with poverty of spirit.

As I retold these stories I began to remember other stories—stories from my own life, stories I'd heard and stories I'd experienced—that authenticated some of these original stories. The modern stories gave me the eyes of faith with which to read the early stories.

For example, we all long for the experience of God in our lives. Then we read how St. Francis embraced a leper and realized he had held God in his arms; and we begin to remember repulsive, difficult times in our own lives that turned out somehow divine. We begin to remember experiences of God's presence that we didn't know were experiences of God's presence until we heard the story of St. Francis and the leper.

That is the way stories work. They remind us of our own stories, and our own stories convince us the original stories are true. And we are then drawn to give thanks to God and to reflect upon our own experience in a more prayerful way. That is why I have included brief reflections and/or prayers at the end of each of the stories, in order to help the reader to begin praying, through the story, about his or her own stories. For the end of all our stories is union with God, and it is prayer which begins to lead us into that union even here on earth, where God's kingdom begins.

In those days, just outside the walls of Assisi, there lived a beautiful lady whom no one knew existed, because she walked about disguised, lest she be discovered and forced to marry against her will. She wanted to marry someone who loved her, someone who had found her out because he had heard her name and seen her face somewhere inside himself. She knew that he would not understand at first who she was or where she lived, but would then recognize her as the lady in his dream, the lady whose hand God had offered him in marriage.

A CHILDHOOD FRIEND

RANCIS and I grew up together in the small town of Assisi in the Valley of Spoleto. Francis was born in 1182, and I, the following year; and I was with him through all the years of his youth.

His family was very rich, but he wasn't snobbish and full of his own self-importance like so many of the other rich sons of Assisi. Rather, he was full of fun and good humor, or at least he was until we all had to go to fight in battle. Francis was twenty years old then, and he was imprisoned and did not return for a year. Before, he used to work with his father, Pietro Bernardone, turning a good profit selling cloth; by night, he joined us as we ganged through the mazelike streets of Assisi, singing and carousing, keeping people awake, and in general making nuisances of ourselves. But though Francis himself was a leader among us obnoxious youth, we noticed that even in his dissipation and endless partying, there was something different about him. He seemed somehow detached from it all, as if he were seeing everything from some high window in his father's house.

After he returned from prison, he didn't party much anymore; and before long, he went off to Spoleto on another one of his pursuits of knighthood. But he returned after a day and a night, and began to seek out lonely places and dark caves to pray in. He was especially drawn to the high woods of Mount Subasio. He would come to my house early in the morning and beg me to go with him to Mount Subasio. And I, because of our friendship, would drag myself out of bed and trudge up the mountain with Francis, only to be left outside, puzzled and a bit resentful, as Francis entered alone into the side of the mountain as into a wound. And when he came out in the evening, Francis himself would look like a wound, so bloody was the battle, or whatever it was that he engaged in, deep in that mountain.

And then one day it was over. Francis emerged from the cave, and to my surprise, he was radiant, as if a man newly fashioned, born again from the mountain's side. And that very night he rejoined us in our rounds of the city.

But Francis began to fall behind the rest of us, and when we noticed him dragging his pace and lingering in the shadows of the moon, we whispered to one another and laughed. Then turning around and putting my hands on my hips, I said in a singsong, mocking tone, "Francis is in lo-ove, Francis is in lo-o-o-ve!" And we all laughed and made unseemly gestures.

But Francis, avoiding the obvious challenge to tell all, only looked at me. Then with a quizzical expression which seemed to indicate that even *he* did not fully know what his words meant, he said, "It's true. And I am going to marry her besides. She is more noble, more beautiful, more wise than any lady you have ever seen."

And from that day on, Francis began to drop farther and farther behind us as we danced and sang through Assisi's streets. And we thought he was lapsing into some strange and

22

fatal sickness. How could we have known that he had seen the face of God? ✦

W HERE IS GOD TODAY? Is he the man who is opening his stall at the farmer's market at the end of the street, a cup of coffee in his hand and a limp cigarette hanging from his mouth? Is she the black lady who raises the piece of oilcloth that serves as a shade over her window? Is he the policeman who drives his cruiser through the lot looking, heaven knows for what, this early in the morning? Or is the face of God all these and more, beckoning me to drop behind my headlong dash into *my* concerns, *my* work, *my* day? Is not prayer like dropping behind awhile to see and hear and touch the God who is talking to me quietly in the fogged faces that clear, as the sun of my pausing illumines what I thought was only another dark morning of routine?

Lord, I know that it is never too late to begin seeing you again, and so I pray that St. Francis will help me drop back from my own selfish pursuits and find you in the faces where you wait.

The Knight Who Inspired St. Francis

RANCIS heard that I, a nobleman of Assisi, was fitting myself out in knightly vesture to go to war in Apulia. Now, Francis had always dreamed of becoming a knight and had in fact gone to battle with the forces of Assisi against Perugia and was taken prisoner at the very onset in a brief skirmish at Ponte San Giovanni, a small village near Perugia. And when he was finally released, he fell into the illness from which he was just rising disillusioned and without his old enthusiasm, when he discovered I was going to Apulia to join the Papal forces of Walter of Brienne.

He was again renewed, energetic, ready to start all over, simply because he had heard of my intention of going to war. "Surely," he said, "yours must be my way in life; for even now, hardly risen from my sickbed, I am ready once again to go into battle."

And the night before we left Assisi, Francis had a dream that seemed to confirm his waking dreams of the glory of knighthood. In the dream, his father's shop was filled with the trappings of knights and soldiers: saddles and armor and lances, instead of the bolts of cloth that usually weighted the shelves. And a voice in the dream answered Francis' amazement with "All of this is for you and your followers."

But when Francis awoke, even though he believed the

dream to be a confirmation of his own deepest desires, he told me that he had to force himself to rise and set out with me to Apulia. Some vague reluctance gnawed at him; and when we stopped for the night in the city of Spoleto, he dreamed the dream that told him what it was.

When he was deep in sleep, Francis heard someone calling him by name, "Francis, Francis! Who can bring you further, the Lord or his servant, the rich man or the beggar?"

And Francis, still asleep, answered, "Why, the Lord, the rich man, to be sure."

"Then why are you following the servant instead of the master, the beggar rather than the Lord, your God? The saddles and weapons of last night's dream are for a spiritual battle, not an earthly one."

And Francis, now alert and listening in his sleep, cried out, "Then, Lord, tell me what that battle is. What is it you want me to do?"

But all that the voice replied was "Return to Assisi at dawn, and there it will be revealed to you what you are to do."

And when Francis awoke at dawn, he saddled up his horse, and to my great dismay, he told me the dream. Then he turned and rode back, even though he still was not certain what all these strange dreams by night and confused feelings by day could mean. ❧

Lᴏʀᴅ Jᴇsᴜs, ʜᴏᴡ ᴍᴀɴʏ and how various are the voices around us and within us. Voices in the press, in our friends. Voices in our dreams. How can we know which ones are from you and which ones are only human voices, some trying to help, some leading us away from you?

The voice St. Francis obeyed was the one that told him to return to his own town, where it would be revealed to him what he should do. Perhaps that is your true voice within me, too, the one beckoning me home to my true self. The way home is the way to my soul, where you are waiting to reveal to me what you want me to do.

Lead me home, Lord. I know you are waiting for me there. I come to you inside, you who are there, you who are my home.

Sᴛ. Fʀᴀɴᴄɪs Mᴇᴇᴛs ᴀ Lᴇᴘᴇʀ

EVERYTHING—the soft mists over the valley of Spoleto, the feeding swallows that rush back and forth in the air, the clear blue skies above the fields of poppies that had always thrilled him before when he looked out across the western end of town toward

Perugia—everything seemed drab and ordinary, and his heart sank into a deep depression. He knew somehow that he had lost his youth, that the glow had vanished from the world, that something in himself was no longer there.

Then one day, as Francis was riding on the road below the city, I suddenly appeared in his way. He reined quickly to the side to gallop past me, a repulsive creature standing there frightened, ringing my small bell, and moving with a twisted, tortured limp to the edge of the road.

But just as Francis was about to veer instinctively around my wretched figure, he forced a sideways glance at my pitiful, upturned face; and he saw that I was a woman. Then something must have jarred in his memory, for as he slid from his horse and began walking unsteadily toward me, he said aloud, "I smell the damp walls of the cave on Mount Subasio, I see Jesus offering me the beautiful feminine hand." Then he came straight to me and started to drop some coins into my hand stretched out in a kind of defensive supplication, an automatic gesture that was the only gesture it knew how to make toward those who were clean.

But Francis took my hand in his own and kissed it and closed into it a gold coin. Then he looked into the face he had always feared seeing and in one swift movement of repulsion and recognition, he kissed my putrefying mouth and knew I was she and felt the rush of love through his whole body. And when he let me go and opened his eyes, he kept saying "Where are you, I can't see you, where have you gone?"

I was still there, but he could not see me because the Lord of All wanted Francis to know that Lady Poverty's

27

true face can never be possessed the way one might think to possess a woman of mere flesh and blood. He would only know me in a brief embrace, and then only when his love grew strong enough to embrace what he found difficult to embrace. He would have to return again and again to the poor and despised and rejected. Only then would he see my countenance fleetingly ringing with light the broken person in his arms. ❧

WE LOOK FOR GOD'S FACE, and it continues to elude us until, like St. Francis, we embrace God in every creature. In that meeting we learn that God's face is both masculine and feminine. It is not always beautiful at first glance. It is often revealed where I least expect to find it. And sometimes, even when God's countenance is revealed to me, I fail to recognize whose face it really is.

Only faith, hope, and love enable me to glimpse the face of God here on earth. And faith and hope are possible only where there is true love.

Lord, I pray that you enlighten my eyes with faith, my will with hope, my heart and mind with love, that I may see the reflection of your image everywhere I look.

FATHER AND SON

HOUGH I was preoccupied with my business, I was aware of the changes that began to alter my son after he returned in ignominy from Spoleto. Francis' heart had never really been in the family business, but the boy had at least been conscientious in helping me in the shop. But after his return home, he seemed more and more distracted and he worked in a perfunctory, distracted manner.

I said nothing, but I began to think that Francis was somehow trying to spite me, and my initial hurt turned into a submerged anger that I knew would eventually explode upon this son of mine, who considered himself better than his father and who looked down upon everything I spent a lifetime building. I had hoped that one day Francis would take over the family business and proudly build upon the foundation I had carefully laid.

And so it began, a bitter and terrible rift between Pietro Bernardone and his son. Neither of us wanted it to happen; neither could keep it from happening.

It is Christ himself—I tremble to say it—who came between Francis and me, and when it finally came to pass, the dreaded confrontation, this is how it was.

Francis burst into the shop and declared he was bringing home a beautiful bride; then he left and returned a few hours later, telling me that he had been out walking near the Church of San Damiano (which he compared to a leper because it lay outside the city walls) and that as he walked along, deep in thought, something moved him to go into the dilapidated church and pray.

As he knelt before the Byzantine cross that hung askew from the arch above the altar he heard, he claimed, a voice coming from the mouth of the painted Christ.

"Francis, don't you see that my house is falling to ruin? Go, then, and repair it for me."

He was struck with amazement, he said, and took these words literally to heart and answered, "Lord, gladly! Gladly will I do it!" Then he fell on his face before the image of the crucified Christ and thanked the Lord for this simple request that Francis, as he said himself, "could easily understand and more easily fulfill."

Then he said he went immediately to the poor priest who had charge of that ramshackle chapel and gave him his purse, saying "Father, please keep this money to buy oil for the lamp that burns before the crucifix. And when you run out of money, I will give you more; for the light before the crucified Christ must never be allowed to burn out."

Then he ran out of the church and up the path to the city, for now he knew what the Lord wanted him to do. Never mind what I, his father, wanted for him, my son.

When Francis arrived at the shop, he ran to one of the shelves and took a bolt of cloth. He bounded down the stairs to the stable, saddled his horse, and rode off to Foligno to sell the cloth for money to rebuild the Church of San Damiano. And not only did my impetuous son sell the cloth, but he found a buyer for the horse as well, so that he returned to Assisi on foot, singing and running for joy. And then he went again to San Damiano, and gave all the money to the startled priest, assuring him it was God's will that the money be used to restore God's house, which was slowly going to ruin.

But the priest, honest man that he is, refused the money, thinking that Francis Bernardone had gone mad and had stolen the money from me, whose reputation for being frugal is well known in Assisi. He insisted that Francis return the money to me, but the boy would not be deterred. He threw the bag of coins on the church's windowsill, and assuring the priest he would return, made his way back to town.

When he returned, I was already livid with rage over the missing cloth and demanded to know why Francis was on foot. Where was the horse I had given him for his birthday, and where was the bolt of taffeta? And when Francis, filled with enthusiasm, eagerly told me again what he had heard from the mouth of the crucified Christ Himself and what he had then done to ensure that Christ's command be promptly carried out, I stood there in utter disbelief. Unable to speak at first, I only grew red with anger as the seconds passed by in silence.

Then, out of sheer frustration and disappointed love, I began to strike my son—God forgive me!—and I threw him into a prisonlike room of the house and bolted the door and ordered my packhorses to be readied for another trip. I would go to France not only to buy cloth but also to clear my mind, to get away for a while and hopefully to determine what to do with this son of mine gone mad with religion.

I ordered my wife, Lady Pica, to keep Francis locked up until my return; but as it is with mothers, even as the last of my packhorses clopped through the city gates, I'm sure she released her son and took him in her arms. And Francis, telling her what he must do, ran down the hill to San Damiano, where, I discovered later, he took up residence and began to restore the church, as the voice had commanded. My own son stooped to begging stones from anyone who would give them to a rich man gone poor with madness. ✤

ONCE THE "FOOLISHNESS OF GOD" has entered the heart, there is no stopping its intoxicating effect upon one's life. Others may try to root it out with reason or laying on of guilt or pleas for sanity, but they only grow weary and frustrated and angry. The foolishness of God is wisdom to those who embrace it, and wisdom, once it enters the heart, is not given up easily.

For St. Francis, wisdom is revealed as Lady Poverty, she who is revealed in the self-emptying of Jesus Christ. St. Francis' reminder to us of the poverty of God is an important corrective in a world that can sometimes identify holiness with material success.

Lord, it is easy to believe in you and see you where there is power and success and riches. It is harder to see you when you are powerless and a failure and poor. And, yet, you are both—the God of power and might, all-powerful and glorious forever, and also the self-emptying God, who does not cling to equality with Godhead but empties himself, becoming as we are, even to accepting death on a cross. Help me to see both your faces, Lord; help me to see that they are really one.

THE POOR PRIEST OF SAN DAMIANO

 AM an old priest and I have come to know that what at first seems madness can become in truth the greatest sanity. And so it is with the way people have come to view Francis, the son of Pietro Bernardone. He has begun to win them over one by one, these skeptical people of his own town. But it was not until his father returned to the city that there occurred an event which was like a gauntlet thrown before the people of Assisi, forcing them to choose whether Francis was mad or somehow blessed.

Pietro returned, and finding the door of his son's imprisonment open and the boy gone, he upbraided his wife and demanded to know where his son had fled. Then one of the servants said, "He lives with the priest at San Damiano," and Pietro hurried down the hill in a rage, uttering curses and swearing that he would receive satisfaction from his son.

33

Francis, in the meantime, fleeing from his father's anger hid in a small cavelike cell here at San Damiano. He could hear his father's rampaging through the church and his importuning of me, but Francis remained hidden. And so it passed, the great scare.

Pietro went home and locked himself up in his house for shame that his son was hiding somewhere like a coward. And Francis, in the meantime, continued to hide in the earth and beg God for courage to face his father's wrath.

Then one day Francis came out of hiding and went up the hill and through the city gates into the jaws of his father's wrath. I followed after him. His father, spotting Francis on the street rushed from his shop, grabbed Francis, and dragged him before the mayor of Assisi. Pietro was a proud Italian father, and Francis was his heart's pride, his son, his flesh. And this flesh had humiliated him.

The crowd that gathered was not immediately sympathetic when Francis revealed that he was, by divine grace, a servant of God and therefore no longer owed obedience to the civil authorities. And so the mayor, infuriated yet wisely wanting to quell a possible riot, sent Francis and his father to the Bishop of Assisi, who agreed to hear Pietro's case.

"My Lord Bishop," Pietro began, "this ungrateful son of mine has defrauded me of some precious cloth and a good horse by selling them without my permission and refusing to return the money that is mine."

"Is this true, Francis? What do you have to say in answer to your father?"

"My Lord, what he says is true. But the horse was mine,

and I gave the money to the Church of San Damiano, and I am now a servant of God."

"Well, Francis, since you claim to be God's servant, I suggest you return your father's money. The cloth was not yours to give away, and the horse, even though your own, was, I'm sure, a gift from your father that should have been appreciated as such."

"My Lord, I no longer have the money, but I'll gladly give back all that is left of my father's goods."

And then Francis stripped himself of his clothes and dropped them like a gauntlet at the feet of his father. It was shocking but at the same time somehow understandable.

"Listen to me, all of you," said Francis softly. "Up till now I have called Pietro Bernardone my father. But from now on I am determined to serve God and say, 'Our Father who art in heaven,' and not 'my father Pietro Bernardone.'"

Francis' words were too terrible to take in, and there was only silence in the courtyard. Then Pietro Bernardone leaned over, picked up the clothes, and, turning away, walked home alone.

Bishop Guido stepped forward and covered Francis' nakedness with his own cloak. And we all walked away in silence, acutely aware that something more than madness had happened before us. ◂

Most of us never have to make such a radical, heartrending break. And, yet, all of us at times make decisions that we know are right and good but make us feel exposed to the critical gaze of others. At those times, we long for some protection, some covering that will insulate our vulnerability and keep us safe enough to persevere in the course we have embarked upon.

Cover me with your cloak, O Lord, for I am afraid of the nakedness I sometimes feel in trying to love you. I am so exposed out here where you've led me. I need to know that your arms surround me. Come, Lord Jesus, and be my tent, my coverlet, shielding me from the eyes of those whose gaze seems at times to penetrate my thin, vulnerable skin.

Of Bernard of Quintavalle, St. francis' First Companion

 S a wealthy and important citizen of Assisi, I was held in great respect by all the townspeople. My house was just a short distance from the Bishop's residence and the courtyard of the Church of St. Mary Major, where Francis had renounced his father. I did not witness the scene myself, but that is all I heard about for weeks from those of my neighbors who did witness it. So, my own curiosity having been enkindled, I began to observe Francis in order to judge for myself what manner of man he was.

I had long been unhappy and lonely in my wealth. I had no wife, no children. Life held no joy for me; yet, that is what I heard about when people talked of Francis—joy. So, I devised a plan whereby I could more closely test Francis' character and see for myself if he was but some eager youth rebelling against society or if it was all true, this personal love of Christ, this joy.

I invited Francis to dinner in order to discern for myself. And this is how it happened that I saw what manner of man Francis was, and Francis saw the manner of man who was to become his first brother.

While we were at supper, I noticed how easy Francis' manner was, how he was not at all self-conscious as he ate heartily away, talking excitedly of his project to restore the Church of San Damiano. He was so convincing that had I been less skeptical, Francis would have convinced me that he was only the bored son of the richest merchant of Assisi, a spoiled young man who needed another kind of diversion. But I saw through Francis' mask of feigned levity and asked Francis to stay the night that I might spend more time with him.

So when it came time to retire, I showed Francis to his bed, a large feather bed that I suspected Francis would shun in favor of the floor. But Francis instead went over to the great bed and lay down upon the soft quilts. Then he turned on his side and closed his eyes.

I had him sleep in my room as a sort of test, to see if he would really stay in my luxurious bed all night or leave it and embrace the floor in secret. In the meantime, I had gone to a cot across the room and lain down, wishing Francis a good night.

But to my surprise there was no response except for the deep breathing of Francis interspersed with catches of snoring. Then I turned and lay on my back and waited for about a quarter of an hour before I, too, began snoring, pretending to be in a deep sleep.

After a half hour or so, I heard a rustling in the other bed; and opening an eye, I could make out the figure of Francis sliding over the edge of the bed onto the floor and kneeling there perfectly still. After a while his mouth began moving slowly.

"My God and my all. My God and my all." Over and over he repeated the same words. I felt mesmerized by the incantatory rhythm of his praying and humbled to be in the presence of someone who had truly renounced what I had so dearly surrounded myself with. It gripped my heart.

All through the night the words continued and I could feel from time to time the hot tears coursing down my own cheeks as I listened to Francis crying in the dark. I tried to focus my soul, to aim the words more accurately, but my bow was warped and my hands shook and I felt bound by cords that fastened me to the bed. I could not rise.

"My God and my all. My God and my all." Suddenly I

knew that was it. God was not my all. God had to become my all, or I would die strapped to my bed.

I no longer heard the words of Francis. I was not listening; I was lost in my own revelation. I knew. I saw it all so clearly. It was not Francis' begging, his poverty, his crazy behavior that mattered. That is not what had drawn me to invite him to supper. It was who God was for him. "My God and my all. My God and my all." That was it. Everything else would fall into place if only I let those words take me where they were leading.

Then I began to pray along with Francis. I tried to enter the words, and I began to feel my hands steadying and my bow straightening as the first dim rays of dawn softened the darkness. I knew I had to get rid of the cords. Only they were holding me back.

I opened my eyes and felt wholly refreshed, renewed, as if I had been sleeping for a long, long time. I leapt from the bed and awakened the startled Francis.

"O Francis, what has God done to me? Here I am fully awake so early in the morning. My mind is clear and I realize that I am somehow completely resolved to leave the world and follow you. What must I do?"

"Bernard, surely these words do not come from you. They are from God. Truly they are of God, so it is to God that we must go to know what he would have you do. Let us go to church. There we will hear Mass and then remain awhile in prayer. Afterward we will ask the priest to open the Holy Gospels and read to us. In the Word of God we will know what it is the Lord wants us to do."

We then went immediately to the Church of St. Nicholas. Francis went directly to the sacristy and asked the priest if he would read the Mass for us, which he did, and afterward he opened the Gospel three times. And these are the words that the Lord revealed to us.

The first words were those of Jesus to the rich young man who asked how he might enter the way of perfection: "If you wish to be perfect, go and sell your possessions, and give the money to the poor and you will have treasure in heaven; then come, follow me" (Mt 19:20). And at the second opening of the book Jesus revealed the words he had spoken to his Apostles when he sent them forth to preach: "Take nothing for the journey; neither staff, nor haversack, nor bread, nor money; and do not have a spare tunic" (Lk 9:3). Francis and I only looked at each other in wonder. Nor were we surprised when at the third opening we heard, "If anyone wants to be a follower of mine, let him renounce himself and take up his cross and follow me" (Mt 16:24).

Then Francis beamed and gave praise to God. And he said to me, "Now we know that it is truly the Lord who has spoken to your heart. And we know clearly what it is he wants of us. Let us do immediately what we both know has to be done."

And I went out and sold all my possessions and, with Francis at my side, began to give away all my money to whoever approached us in the Piazza del Comune. ✢

LOOKING CLOSELY. That is the beginning of prayer. And it is as true of looking at those around me as it is, say, of looking at a crucifix or a painting of Christ. For Christ is revealed in those who are his mirror. Bernard of Quintavalle saw in Francis a reflection of the living God because he took the time to really look at Francis.

Someone once said, "If you look long enough at anything, it will finally look back at you." The result of this contemplative looking is that we finally see that everything which exists has meaning, has some gift to offer us if we would only look long enough, look properly. But reflections can be distorted and images can be reversed. Therefore, we must come with reverence and humility, surrendering to the true face of the gift that the Giver has given.

THE PRIEST WHO BECAME BROTHER SYLVESTER

EEDLESS to say, there was a great stir among the people of Assisi, and a large crowd gathered in the Piazza del Comune when the wealthy Bernard of Quintavalle poured coins into the outstretched hands of the poor, of orphans and widows, of pilgrims, and

TALES OF ST. FRANCIS

whoever else stretched out their hands, including those who were not poor, like me, the priest Sylvester, who heard of this prodigality and approached Bernard and Francis as they stood casting coins into the air.

"Francis, how can you throw money away like this when you know you still owe me money for the stones I gave you for the repair of San Damiano? Surely you don't think the pittance you offered in return was sufficient pay for all the stones I procured?"

And Francis said, "Oh no, Father Sylvester. In fact, I was so hoping you'd come. Here is your money."

Then Francis dug deep into Bernard's lap and poured a whole handful of coins into my greedy palms.

"Thank you, Francis. Thank you, Bernard. I knew you would not cheat a poor priest."

But I could not sleep that night and the next and the next, except for a very brief time during which I dreamed that from the mouth of Francis there issued a cross of gold, and the top of it reached to heaven, and the arms stretched from the east all the way to the west. When I awoke I was in a cold sweat, knowing that I had cheated God by taking Bernard's money from the hands of the truly poor. And because of this, I repented and gave away all that I had for the love of God and went to Francis to ask him to forgive me and teach me the ways of a Lesser Brother.

Like Bernard, I had changed. And I persevered to the end with such holiness that Francis said of me that I spoke with God as does one friend with another. And that is how Francis found Bernard and how the two of them found me, the second companion.

It was not long after this that Francis and Bernard and I were joined by Giles, a good, holy man of Assisi. We lived a life of love—love of God and love of one another. We cared for one another spiritually and physically, as a mother loves and cherishes the child of her womb. And when we grew an additional seven in number and Francis saw that we were now eleven like the Apostles after the Resurrection, he drew up a Rule of Life and decided to go to Rome in order to ask the Pope himself to approve our way of life and sanction our preaching of penance.

And so Francis and the rest of us set off to see the Holy Father, with Brother Bernard appointed by Francis to act as our leader along the way. Whatever road Bernard said we should take, we were to all obey, and wherever he said we were to stop for the night to beg for food and to sleep, we were to obediently comply. And so, like the great Apostles Peter and Paul, we made our way to Rome on foot, sometimes singing, sometimes silent, but always praying. And when we entered the Holy City, we found the Bishop of Assisi there, and he at first was saddened by our presence in Rome; for he admired us and thought that we were forsaking Assisi for Rome.

But when he learned the nature of our visit, he rejoiced and arranged an audience with the Pope for us through the great and powerful Cardinal John of St. Paul. And Francis rejoiced in turn, for he had often consulted with Bishop Guido of Assisi before his conversion to the Lord, and the bishop had always provided good advice and practical help as when he had covered Francis' nakedness with his own cloak. And even here, outside the protective walls of Assisi,

43

it was Bishop Guido who came to his aid. Surely the good bishop was an angel of mercy, and we thanked and praised the Lord for sending his messenger to help us. ❧

F~EW OF US HAVE VISIONS~ and dreams like Brother Sylvester's or like St. Francis' himself. But we do see people who have been changed dramatically into people in love with God, spending themselves in God's service. And perhaps it has already happened that someone's life or death has changed our own way of living, someone like Mother Teresa of Calcutta or the martyred Bishop Oscar Romero, or someone less famous, someone perhaps known only to us.

Lord, let the quiet example of saintly lives move me to large conclusions in my own life. I feel overwhelmed in comparison to your great saints. Let me be small, but let me be holy. Let me understand what you brought the French novelist Léon Bloy to understand—"There is only one tragedy, not to be a saint."

THE POOR WOMAN WHO LIVED
IN THE DESERT

I T happened in God's Providence that Francis and his brothers came before me, Pope Innocent III, who received these brothers of penance gladly. I listened with joy to their request to live the Gospel more fully and I sent them forth to preach repentance to the people. But when they were leaving my presence, I called them back and asked them to pray that they might know with certainty whether the poverty they proposed to live was of God. For though their poverty was of truth the poverty of Christ's Gospel, I wondered at its severity and whether it could or really would be lived after the first glow of the brothers' profession of poverty grew dim. And what about those who were to come after them? Would such a radical poverty endure the passage of time, the passing of the charismatic Francis?

Such were my concerns, and Francis took them most seriously to the Lord and begged God to give me cause to be at peace and know that it was the Lord, who had inspired Francis to live a life of Holy Gospel poverty. And as Francis prayed, the Lord revealed to him a parable and had him come and tell it to me.

And this is what he said: There was a very beautiful but poor woman who lived in the desert, and the king, hearing of her beauty and going to visit her, saw that she was truly as beautiful as she was rumored to be. Therefore, he determined to marry her and had the marriage contract drawn up immediately. Through her, the king had many sons and then returned to his palace. And when the sons grew up and the mother had nothing to give them by way of inheritance, she told them not to be ashamed of their poverty, for they were the sons of the king. The sons then went to the king's palace, and when he saw them, he saw their resemblance to himself and asked who they were. "We are the sons of the poor woman of the desert," they said. And the king rejoiced and welcomed them as his own.

Now, when Francis told me this parable, I was much amazed, especially when he concluded with, "And I, Holy Father, am the woman of the desert."

I marveled at Francis' simplicity and at the impact this little beggar's story had made upon me. Then I remembered a dream I had had, a few nights before, of the great Church of St. John Lateran, the mother church of all Christendom, falling to the ground and a small man supporting the falling building with his shoulder. And I suddenly realized that Francis was the man in my dream.

I then stepped down from my throne and embraced him and his brothers and ordered that they all be tonsured as clerics so that they could preach penance in the name of God and the Church. And I sent them on their way. ✤

St. Francis' parable of the poor woman of the desert reveals how uninhibited and comfortable he is with the feminine side of his personality, with his soul. He does not hesitate to proclaim his mothering of the Order that God is bringing to birth through him. Francis sees clearly that we are all feminine before God. We are brides of Christ and we are made fruitful in God's embrace. We are pregnant with God and bring forth virtue and goodness through God, whose Spirit has overshadowed us, God's mothers. It is we who bring forth God in our time, but we must first let him embrace us.

As St. Francis himself wrote in his letter to All the Faithful, "We are his spouses when our faithful souls are wed to Jesus Christ by the Holy Spirit. . . . We are mothers of our Lord Jesus Christ when we carry him in our hearts and in our bodies, lovingly, and with a pure and sincere conscience. We give birth to him through the working of his grace in us, which should shine forth as an example to others."

THE ANGEL OF POGGIO BUSTONE

OGGIO Bustone is a very humble village; still, its people, who are poor and hardworking, love their village, which hangs precariously on the side of a mountain above Rieti. They do not consider themselves less than those others of Greccio, on the opposite mountain, or even those of Rieti, the larger city on the plain.

But there was a time when these people did not know that God's goodness was greater than their sins. At this time Francis felt he was full of sin too, and he happened to come to Poggio Bustone filled with a like despair and conviction that his sins were unforgivable.

But even though he felt dark and depressed as he entered the town, Francis struggled to set aside his own feelings and to say something that would make the waking citizens feel good about themselves again. He hoped the words would begin to change the way he felt too.

What he said was "Good morning, good people."

And the people were dumbfounded. No one had ever said as much to them, at least not publicly and on a bright fall morning just as winter was beginning to descend on them. And what's more, he shouted it aloud over and over again as he walked through their streets, this little barefoot man and the six bedraggled companions who trudged along behind him!

Who was he? And whatever did he mean by calling them good when their priest had warned them that God alone is good? And what's more, this stranger called them good in the same breath with the morning itself: "Good morning, good people!"

Francis himself was surprised by the words that sprang spontaneously to his lips, for he had never used such a greeting before. Yet, somehow he knew how good these people were, how good the world was. And what these people already were, he was about to become, in this very place: good. He did not know how, but he knew it, and it would be a new and good morning in his life.

And this is how it happened: There was a small cave high above the mountain village, and Francis was drawn there as to the rising sun itself. Even at a distance, that spot on the mountain seemed ringed in light. Now, never in his wildest imaginings would Francis have guessed that the light was mine, an angel sent by God to assure him and all who would see and hear him from that day forward, that God is bigger than human sins and that it is people themselves who are too small to forgive themselves. They think God is overwhelmed, like them, by the greatness of their sins, but that is only human pride in thinking God is limited in mercy like them and that He needs to take out His vengeance on them the way they need to take it out on themselves for being imperfect, human, not angelic.

That is what I was waiting to say to Francis as he scurried up the mountain toward the light, his followers stumbling behind him, almost as if they were pushing the load of sins that Francis was dragging behind him. So conscious was he of his sins and how grievous they had been when he was in the world lusting for the bloody business of knighthood and war that sin was all he could see, sin in him and around him, sin in the world, sin in his own soul.

And that is why it was so surprising that the first thing he should say when entering Poggio Bustone was "Good morning, good people," and the first thing he should see on the mountain was a bright light. How strange! How extraordinary! And yet, that is how it was.

But the surprise waiting for Francis in the cave was even greater; for when he entered the ring of light, he saw me there, and I appeared as a beautiful woman! I assured him

all his sins were indeed forgiven, and Francis suddenly felt
he was being born again through this angelic woman. Then
he thought of the woman whose face he could not see, of
the leper, of the bride in his dreams, of the poor woman of
the desert, of Mary, the Mother of Jesus. And all these
women came together in the image of the Virgin Mary that
rose from his heart, and he began to sing her praises:

> I salute you, holy Lady,
> Most holy Queen,
> Mother of God, Mary.
> You are Virgin made Church,
> Chosen one of the most holy Father of heaven,
> Consecrated by him together with his most holy,
> Beloved Son, with the Holy Spirit, the Paraclete.
> In you there was and is every fullness of grace
> and every good.
> Hail, his Palace, his Tent, his House, his Clothing.
> Hail, his Maidservant, his Mother.
> And Hail all you holy Virtues, who through
> the grace and light of the Holy Spirit permeate the
> hearts of the faithful, rendering those who were once
> faithless, faithful to God.

Woman, Mary, Virtues, Light. They were all one womb of
God and for God in the vision that flooded Francis' soul at
Poggio Bustone, and he walked from the cave like a new
morning, fresh and good like the people of Poggio Bustone. ❧

How OFTEN WE FEEL that somehow we don't measure up, that we are imperfect, or even at times evil. In our time especially, we are given to endless introspection and self-scrutiny. We analyze ourselves and ask others to analyze us. We submit ourselves to every kind of program to ferret out each particle of darkness and self-deception. But to what end if the Lord is not there affirming us with love? Self-scrutiny only leads to self-hatred if it is performed apart from what the angel announced to Francis—that all his sins were forgiven. I cannot absolve myself. Only God can, and God does, all the days of my life.

Lord, you have said to me, "You are light for the world; you are salt for the earth." I do believe that and I do believe that you love me and have forgiven me; I believe you dwell within me. Help me, then, never to minimize my own goodness, especially when I am down on myself. Help me to see and build upon what is good and positive about me rather than upon the negative, which I am all too ready to notice. Lord, help me, for how hard it is to have faith and hope in your mercy and how easy it is to despair.

THE HUNGRY BROTHER AND RIVO TORTO

HERE was a time, near the beginning, when Francis and the rest of us brothers lived at a place near Assisi called Rivo Torto. It was called Rivo Torto because of the twisting river that flowed there, and it became for us a river paradise. For there, beside the banks of the river, we lived our first idyllic months with Lady Poverty, the true Novice Mistress of the Order of St. Francis. The hut we lived in was so cramped that Francis had to write our names on the beams so that each brother would have an assigned place for praying and sleeping.

At Rivo Torto we fasted and did penance with all the enthusiasm and sometimes the imprudence of novices in the life of the Spirit, as the following story shows.

One night, as all lay sleeping soundly, my loud cry broke into the brothers' dreams.

"I am dying! I am dying! Help me!" I cried.

And the brothers, startled from their sleep, saw Francis already at my side.

"What is it, brother? Tell me."

And though I was now embarrassed, I overcame my shame and said, "Forgive me, Father Francis, but I am dying of hunger."

Then Francis immediately ordered the brothers to light a torch and go out and gather some herbs and vegetables and whatever else they could find for all of us to have a good, nourishing meal. He said this so that I would not have to be humiliated by eating alone. And so all the brothers set themselves eagerly to the task of preparing a meal and then they all sat down with me and ate a midnight supper.

But when we had finished, Francis admonished us all, saying "My brothers, in all the fasting and penance you do for the love of our Lord Jesus Christ, you must always take your own constitution into consideration and give your body what it needs. You must avoid excessive mortification in the same way that you avoid excessive eating and drinking. For it is not the food that is sinful or the lack of food that is virtuous. Rather it is the excess that leads to sin and the moderation that enables you to persevere in penance, and it is true self-knowledge that enables you to know what is excessive and what is prudent in your own particular case."

At Rivo Torto there were days of hard work in the fields and nights of prayer and sleeping on the cold ground, and all the while we continued to learn the limits of fasting and penance. And we would have stayed there much longer than we did, had something not happened that drove us forever from the lovely place near the bend of the river of paradise.

Late one afternoon, when we were all at prayer in the little hut, there was a great din and a loud braying outside. And then to our surprise and dismay, a peasant came backing into the hut pulling his reluctant jackass with him and saying "Come on, long ears, here we can at last be comfortable."

It was then that Francis suddenly realized that we had made a home, a comfortable dwelling even out of this hut; and he knew we would have to move on. For soon someone else would want to move in with his animals, and another with his family, and we would keep building additions to the little hut, and pretty soon there would be a village, and we would put up a wall and start excluding people we did not want to live with. Then we would be like monks and not like poor, wandering preaching brothers who, like their Lord and Master, have nowhere to lay their heads. Francis said we must never become so domestic and comfortable that someone like this peasant would want to move in with us in order to dwell in comfort.

So Francis stood up before us and said, "Brothers, I am sure that God has not called us to keep a hotel for asses, but to pray and show others the way to salvation."

Then, just as the peasant had led the ass into the hut and laid claim to it, so Francis led us brothers out the same narrow door into the freedom of the fields, and we never returned to Rivo Torto again. ❧

ONE OF THE DANGERS of experiencing the consolation or presence of God is that we will go to any extreme to hold on to it. We want that experience to remain with us at all costs, not realizing that to live by faith is to let go of God when God wants to withdraw a felt presence. We mature when we let God come and go as God wills and not try to force God to stay by exaggerated penance or poverty or sealing God into our narrow little Rivo Torto of a hut.

Lord, I do not always feel your presence, and I do not see or hear you, but I do believe you are as near to me as my own breath; I believe you dwell within me as intimately as my breath, which I cannot see but which keeps me alive, just as you do.

THE BENEDICTINES OFFER FRANCIS A CHURCH

HE pull of the hearth is stronger than we sometimes realize, and it is there even in a great saint like Francis. For no sooner had the brothers left Rivo Torto than Francis came to us and asked us if we had a shelter that they could make into a home. As abbot, I, Maccabeo, realized full well the position Francis was in; having others in your spiritual charge is not an easy responsibility, particularly when the life was as radically poor as that of Francis and his brothers.

And so, though we lived in monasteries, I was not one to try and change Francis' mind. He was a mystic, like Benedict himself, and had similar communications with God. Such men should be heard, for surely God has many things to say to us who often fail to hear our own neighbor's plea, let alone God's.

We decided to give Francis our poorest church, a little chapel in the fields, which pilgrims from the Holy Land built in the year 352. This chapel of St. Mary of the Angels, which we called the Portiuncula, or Little Portion, would enable the brothers to live in the forest that surrounded the church, and Francis was well pleased with this, so long as we kept ownership of the church and only lent it to them for their use. And in order that it would not eventually become their own from long use, Francis insisted that every year the brothers send us a basket of fish in payment of the rent.

And so they found a hearth. And from our perch on Mount Subasio we watched with loving eyes as they sent each other out in pairs to all the corners of the earth and returned to share their stories, which we heard, and were made part of through the blessing of God. ⁌

WHAT IS MY CENTER, the place or space I retreat to in order to find again the source of all my comings and goings?

St. Francis used to say that we carry our hermitage cell with us, but he also had favorite "outer" places of prayer and contemplation, places like the Portiuncula, the Carceri on Mount Subasio, his mountain retreat of La Verna. He even visited St. Benedict's mountain cave at Subiaco where a fresco, painted by one of the monks, still stands.

Lord, I know I carry a cell with me. But often I need an

outer retreat as well, to remind me of the place within. Comings and goings. Never staying in one place too long, lest the other be forgotten. Lord, let me always have a pilgrim heart.

LADY CLARE OF ASSISI

WAS a young girl when I first heard about Francis. But only when he began to change did I begin to notice him. I was then seventeen years old, and Francis was twenty-eight.

Even before I began to take note of the Lord's work in his life, I had felt the Lord working in mine. I had declined any proposal of marriage that my father, Favarone, had attempted to arrange. Instead, I was content to sew and study Latin, read tales of chivalry, and listen to minstrels in our palazzo, all of which were available to me because I was of the noble house of Offreduccio.

That was the public image, Favarone's much courted daughter. But something else was going on in my soul. When I was alone, I gave myself to prayer and fasting, and I secretly gave food and alms to the poor. At night, when all were asleep, I would spend hours on my knees praying to the Lord for light to know his will for me. And then I heard of Bernardone's son, Francis, and the strange turn of events in his life and how he had begun to live with the lepers on the road below the city.

One day I rode up to the ruins of the fortress above the city and looked down across the plain toward the church of the Portiuncula, where Francis and his brothers were, and I knew I had to be with them.

So I arranged to meet Francis for counsel, but he in turn went immediately to Bishop Guido to ask *his* counsel, because the bishop spoke with God's authority and because I was of a noble house, and my father and my uncle Monaldo, who was the feudal chief, would not take kindly to what was about to happen. But, as he had done when Francis renounced his father, the good bishop told Francis to be steadfast in his resolve. Then the bishop summoned me, and it was decided I should leave my home secretly the night of Palm Sunday, March 18, with my cousin Pacifica, since she was determined to join me in this holy enterprise.

And so on Palm Sunday in the year of Our Lord 1212, I, Clare, the noble daughter of Favarone and Ortolana, went with my parents to the Cathedral of San Rufino for the Solemn Mass commemorating Christ's entry into Jerusalem to prepare for his Passion, Death, and Resurrection. But realizing I might never see my parents again and yet eager to rush with swift feet toward my Beloved, I was overcome with emotion and was unable to rise from my seat and go to the altar to receive the palm. But Bishop Guido, understanding what I was feeling, came down to where I sat and placed the palm in my hand.

That night Pacifica and I fled the house and sneaked quietly past the city guards down the hill to the Portiuncula, where Francis and the brothers were waiting for us. The light of their candles made little moons of the brothers' faces, and we were filled with joy. Francis cut off our hair and clothed us in a coarse habit like the brothers' and led us by candle light to the Benedictine monastery of San Paolo, two miles away in the marshlands of Isola Romana.

When it was discovered that I was living in a monastery with my cousin Pacifica, there was consternation in the house of Offreduccio, and to make matters worse, my younger sister Agnes, who was only fifteen years old, was secretly preparing to join me and Pacifica as a Poor Lady of Jesus Christ too. While all this turmoil was brewing, Francis, Bernard, and Philip had secretly removed me and Pacifica to another Benedictine monastery, Sant'Angelo on the slope of Mount Subasio. There, a week after Easter, Agnes joined us, and Francis himself cut off her hair and received her profession.

Then the anger of our family erupted, and our uncle Monaldo came storming up to Mount Subasio with his knights. At first, he tried to be conciliatory, but when we resisted, he ordered one of the knights to seize Agnes and carry her away. But Agnes resisted violently, beating against the mailed knight with her fists and screaming for me to help as she was dragged down the mountain, her clothing tearing on branches and clumps of her remaining hair catching on bushes and ripping out. Then I knelt and prayed fervently to the Lord, who had led us to Francis, and as I prayed, Agnes became heavier and heavier, as if she had eaten stones, and the knight, who could no longer carry her, dropped her to the ground. One of the other knights then jumped from his horse and was about to strike my terrified sister with his fist, when his arm froze in the air and he could not move it.

Frustrated, then, and fuming with anger, the protectors of the House of Offreduccio had to give up the fight and descend the mountain in defeat. Just then the moon came out from behind a cloud, and I knew we would now be left alone.

Four months later, at Francis' request, Bishop Guido gave us Poor Ladies the Church of San Damiano. And we came to live there, thus fulfilling the prophecy Francis had made when he was rebuilding it: "Someday this place will be the home of Holy Virgins of Christ." ❧

THE NAME CLARE MEANS "bright" and "clear" in Italian. It is fitting that such a light shone for forty years from San Damiano. The twenty years St. Clare lived after the death of St. Francis, she lived in continual sickness, yet she knew Francis was there consoling her and inspiring her, in the stones, the walls, the very mortar around her mat. And more important, the light that Christ became in her continued to grow, radiating beyond the walls.

Lord, such light! It seems incredible that such a clear ray pierced history so completely, like a laser whose source lies within. Fill my vaulted spaces with such love, such radiance, so that like St. Clare, I may shine with you and in you and for you, Lord.

THE WOLF OF GUBBIO

EING a wolf, I was greatly feared and hunted, for I did indeed gnash my teeth and attack many oxen and sheep and occasionally a human or two. I became part of a battle between man and beast. I was a ravenous, larger-than-life wolf so terrifying to the citizens of Gubbio that they were afraid to leave the gates of the city; and if they did leave, they always went armed.

My fame spread through Umbria—even the thirty kilometers to Assisi, where a beggar named Francis, out of compassion for the people of Gubbio and for me as well (so he later told me), set out to find me. But when he reached Gubbio, the people, though they knew the holiness of Francis, weren't very helpful in their fear and warned him against leaving the city gates in search of their wolf. Leave them he did, however, and with no helmet or shield other than a companion and the sign of the cross. He put all his trust in the Creator, who enables all who believe to walk without harm on viper and asp and to lie down not only with wolves like me but also with lions and dragons.

And so it was that Francis and his companion came out to meet me. Many of the townspeople were watching from hiding places where they had climbed to see Francis, like a knight of Christ, go to slay the evil wolf. Nor did they have to wait long, for when the saint was but a short distance from the city gates, I came charging out from within a grove of olive trees and rushed at the two men with open mouth and flashing teeth.

Francis, in return, raised his arm and met me with the sign of the cross, which checked my charge and closed my mouth.

"Brother Wolf," he said, "in the name of Jesus Christ, I command you not to harm me, nor anyone else."

And at those words the terrible wolf I was disappeared, and a gentle, friendly wolf emerged within me and I approached the saint and lay like a lamb at his feet, hardly recognizing myself.

Then the Lord revealed to Francis that I was but a sign and that the real wolf was inside the people of Gubbio, though they saw it outside themselves in me. And when Francis looked about him, the people were indeed looking in amazement at the meek animal I'd become as I lay at Francis' feet.

Thereupon, Francis started talking to me, "Brother Wolf, you have done much harm, not only destroying creatures of God without mercy, but devouring women and men, too, who are made in the image of God. But though you do indeed deserve to be punished, the Lord wants you to make peace with all His creatures instead."

And the people understood that violence like a wolf's does pervert the image of God that we are, and can maim and destroy other creatures. And yet, as he does with them, God offers repentance to the wolf, too, rather than punishment without recourse. And those who looked around and listened to Francis reported that they saw me approach the saint and, in receiving my forgiveness, place my large right paw gently into St. Francis' open palm. And Francis gently shook my paw and released it. He asked me never again to harm the citizens of Gubbio or their animals or people or beasts in any of the surrounding country. Then once again, as if in pledge, I placed my paw into Francis' hand.

And with that, Francis and I, tame as a friendly pet dog, walked into the city square, where, with me at his feet, the saint preached a wondrous sermon in which he told the people that the scourge of the wolf had come upon them because of their sins.

"Return then, dear people, to the Lord and do penance, and God will free you from the wolf. And as a pledge of your repentance, I ask you to embrace Brother Wolf, and give so tame and gentle a creature, his daily bread. And if you do this, I give you the Lord's promise that you will have peace."

And so it happened. For two years I had a pretty interesting life begging from door to door, sometimes looking like a poor beggar, sometimes like a ragged animal; and the people gave me my due. I became Brother Wolf in their hearts and in their lives until the day I died. Then the people mourned for me and for the symbol of their own redeemed violence that I had become. And they vowed to remember that even wolves can be tamed by love, wolves like me and wolves like them. ❧

Wʜᴀᴛ ɪs ᴡɪʟᴅ ᴀɴᴅ ᴠɪᴏʟᴇɴᴛ within us asks us to name it Brother or Sister and to give it the food of charity to satisfy its hunger. For that which seeks to destroy and devour is really hungry for something more than food, something that only "real" food can begin to tame.

Lord, how much violence is the result of need and deprivation. Let me not forget to give. And let me not forget to treat those I give to as my own brothers or sisters, giving to them from my want and not just my excess. Let my bread be real, in consolation, friendship, a visit to the sick. And let me not forget to attend to what is wild in myself. It, too, needs the bread of my charity, my embrace, to transform its violence into creative service in your name.

Sᴛ. Dᴏᴍɪɴɪᴄ ᴀɴᴅ
ᴛʜᴇ Cʜᴀᴘᴛᴇʀ ᴏꜰ Mᴀᴛs

I N 1209, Pope Innocent III verbally approved Francis' Rule of Life. And within seven or eight years there were already some five thousand brothers in the Order. And even though their number was so large, Francis continued to gather them all together at

St. Mary of the Angels on the Feast of Pentecost. There they would confess their faults to one another, tell their stories, and hear his consoling words.

"My dear brothers," he would say, "we have promised great things, but still greater things are promised us. Keep your promises, then, and aspire toward those promises made to us. Pleasure is brief, punishment eternal. Suffering is brief, glory without end. And let none of you be concerned or anxious about food or any other need of the body, but rather concentrate wholly on prayer and the praise of God, casting all your care on Jesus Christ, who has a special care for us."

Now I, Dominic, was visiting at this Chapter of Mats, so called because of the screen of rush matting Francis and his brothers used for shelter, and I thought Francis' exhortation to his brothers was imprudent advice, for I was convinced that if they did not heed the necessities of the body, a dire situation would surely develop among them. But just as I was thinking this, people from Assisi and all the adjacent cities came with donkeys, mules, and horses all loaded with bread and wine, beans and cheese, and everything else they thought Francis and the brothers might need. Seeing this I knelt and begged Francis' forgiveness for doubting the wonderful Providence of God, who always cares for the poor and the little ones of the earth.

And at that same chapter, Francis discovered that many of the brothers were wearing iron breastplates and rings against their skin, so that some were becoming ill or were too weak to pray. He commanded them under obedience to take off these instruments of torture and penance. And to his amazement, there were some five hundred breast-plates and leg and arm rings among them. These he ordered gathered in a huge pile and left there on the plain.

And then Francis preached on what true penance is. He reminded us that the Lord will say to those who have known, served, and adored him in true penance, "Come, you whom my Father has blessed, take for your heritage the kingdom prepared for you since the foundation of the world." And then, lest we misunderstand and think that penance is wearing iron breastplates or rings against the skin, he explained the way of penance that the Lord had shown to him. He spoke to us the words that he later had written down in his testament: "This is the way the Lord granted me, Brother Francis, to begin to do penance. While I was in sin, it seemed bitter to look upon lepers. And the Lord himself led me among them and I worked together with them. And when I left them, what had seemed bitter to me was now changed into sweetness of soul and body for me." ✥

St. Francis used to say that he and the brothers had a contract with the world. If the brothers were faithful to Gospel poverty, the people of God would care for their needs, as St. Dominic saw happen at the Chapter of Mats. Not everyone can live as poorly as St. Francis and the early friars did, but we can all live that Gospel poverty which entails loving those who are not easily loved. In loving what we find difficult to embrace, we are transformed, our thinking is turned around, and we find God. True penance then, is repentance, turning around from self-centeredness to God-centeredness from depending on myself to depending on God.

Lord, teach me poverty of spirit, which depends on you to do what I cannot do. To be poor means to depend on you for everything. To be poor means that I am rich only in what you do in me and for me.

THE MISERABLE LEPER'S TALE

I CURSED God when I became a leper. I cursed God's mother and heaped abuses on God's "servants"—these brothers who came to wash my sores. Why shouldn't I despise them? If God is God, why didn't he heal me? What woman, what mother, would love me, sick and putrid as I am? And these robed servants, ha! They have their health, why do they come and remind me of my misery? I almost got rid of them once and for all until they sent their "father" to me.

"God give you peace, dearest brother," he said.

But I replied as usual, "What peace is there for me? Can't you see that your God has taken away my peace and left me rotten from head to foot?"

"Oh, dear friend, if you only knew what peace awaits you. The sufferings you carry in your body will result in the salvation of your soul, if you bear them in peace."

"But how is this possible," I replied, "when my torture goes on day and night? And not only am I plagued with illness, but I am treated harshly by your brothers who are supposed to be taking care of me."

Then Francis, knowing his brothers had only been loving and kind to me, saw by the grace of the Holy Spirit that I was tortured in spirit also, just as the brothers had suspected, so he went away and prayed devoutly to God.

When he returned, he said, "My son, since you are not satisfied with my brothers, I will serve you myself."

"Is that supposed to make me happy? What can you do that the others have not already tried?"

"I will do whatever you wish."

"Then I want you to give me a bath because I cannot bear my own stench."

Immediately Francis had water heated as he personally began to remove my wretched rags. He then washed me with his hands, while another brother poured water over me. And as I began to be cleansed of dirt, I began to be cleansed of my leprosy, in body and in soul. I saw my body being healed, but I also saw myself anointed and healed in spirit. And I then broke into loud sobs of remorse.

"Oh, sir," I cried, "I am surely worthy of hell for everything I've done to your brothers, for the blows I've dealt them, and for my impatience and blasphemy against God!"

For fifteen days I carried on like this with tears and

extraordinary wailing, seeking only the mercy of God. Then with much weeping, I confessed my sins to a priest. And the peace Blessed Francis had promised was given to me.

Francis, however, because of my healing, had to leave for a while to a far country, lest he be besieged by the curious and those who would run to him when the news of the healing began to spread, for there were thousands of us lepers longing to be healed. Francis wanted no honor; he was a good servant, who only rendered glory and honor to God, keeping only shame and ignominy for himself.

Now shortly after these extraordinary events, I fell ill and died in the grace of God.

Francis, in the meantime, was praying in a forest when he saw before him a man whose light was more resplendent than the sun.

"Sir, do you recognize me? I am the leper whom the Blessed Christ healed through your hands. Today I go to the realm of the blessed, for which I thank Almighty God and you. Blessed be your soul and body, your words and works, for through you many souls are being saved and shall be saved. And know that every day the angels and saints give thanks for the holy fruits you and your Order reap on earth. Be comforted then, and thank God that you are so blessed by Him."

At this, I disappeared, my soul on its way to heaven. ✦

O LORD, HOW MUCH OF MY DOUBTING, my disappointment with you comes from the sickness and suffering I experience in my own life and in the lives of others. It is so hard to believe in you when you seem to do nothing to heal the sick I am praying for. And yet, I know with St. Francis that

69

you do heal sickness and that sickness can lead to health and peace of soul, even if the body is not healed. I have seen it happen and I praise you for it.

I know, too, Lord, that I am your hands in this world, and yet I hold back. I don't reach out and touch those who are sick. I don't pray over them as I should. Perhaps what is lacking is not the divine, but the human touch.

Brother Masseo's Tale

RANCIS preferred me above all the others when he went begging. He would bend over with laughter as I tried desperately to keep the housewives from giving me the choicest morsels and begging me to come inside and have just a glass of wine with them—and all this as they dumped some slop into Francis' open hands, not even looking at him but keeping their eyes fixed on me. You see, I was tall and handsome and eloquent, and Francis was small and rather plain.

And how I would blush with embarrassment that I was being preferred to the man I loved and admired above everyone else.

But Francis would only laugh the deep, hearty laugh of one who sees the real comedy of life, the humor inside the seriousness with which we try to elevate many things into something sublime. Begging, after all, is not sublime; it is demeaning and small, and actually quite ugly. And the only reason Francis insisted on it was that it enabled him and his brothers to feel the Incarnation the way God felt it, for God had come among us as a beggar, his hands open, asking us humbly to receive Him.

Everyone was expecting Jesus to be a Brother Masseo and kept giving their love and affection to the likes of Masseo, so that when Jesus really did come among them, they did not recognize him because of all the Masseos they mistook him for. But I knew I was not God, and after my first embarrassments, learned to laugh even more heartily than Francis, and at times the housewives thought I was laughing at them, which made Francis and me laugh even harder. And then the housewives, too, began to laugh, and everyone began to see how silly we all are and how little and insignificant is God's human appearance, and then our laughter would turn to tears and we would find ourselves— Francis and I and countless good women—kneeling in the middle of the street or raising the worst of the begged food to heaven like a chalice and weeping for the Poor God, whose stench we had suddenly recognized.

And then Francis and I would move on to some other city where laughter had not yet grown deep enough to become grateful tears of love.

But it was not just as a foil that Francis liked to have me with him, nor was it that my charismatic presence reminded Francis of his own littleness and insignificance— although Francis valued that reminder highly, for he knew that it is only through our weakness that the power of God

71

works. No, not for these reasons was I a favorite companion of Francis, but for something else that Francis saw in me and that the following story reveals.

Once when Blessed Francis and I were on the road preaching the Gospel by the example of our love and courtesy, we came to a crossroads that led in three directions—to Florence, Siena, and Arezzo. So I asked Francis, "Father, which way shall we take?"

Now, instead of immediately grasping at the position of power and importance that had just been given him, Francis said, "The way God wishes."

"And how are we to know that?" I asked.

"Well, let me show you, dear brother. In the name of holy obedience, start turning round and round in the middle of the road, the way children do, and don't stop until I tell you."

Then without any questions, I immediately began spinning around in the middle of the road, and I became so dizzy I fell down. But as Francis said nothing, I got up again and began whirling around with renewed vigor, and when I was really picking up speed and my arms were flailing around in the air, Francis suddenly said, "Stop right there, Masseo!"

I stopped cold and asked, "Right where, Father Francis?"

"Which way is your face pointed?"

"Toward Siena."

"Then it is to Siena that God wants us to go!"

And off we went, praising God and congratulating each other on our good fortune in knowing God's will, which so few people know with such surety.

And this, then, is why Francis loved to go through the world with me: I never put any limits on the amount of silliness I would tolerate in others. In fact, I relished Francis' most outlandish requests. And thus it was that Francis was sure of knowing God's will through me, for whom human foolishness became the wisdom of God. And because I was willing to submit to the seemingly foolish and silly things Francis asked of me out of holy obedience, the wisdom of God was made manifest in my responses. And Francis could then be sure that we were not acting from self-interest, or the will to power, or human wisdom, but out of our own foolishness made wise by submitting it to God's discernment. ❧

LORD, HOW MANY TIMES I have seen others as "gods" or rivals because they were stronger or more beautiful or more popular than I! If only I had the eyes of St. Francis to see all the Masseos of my life as who they really are—just one tiny reflection of you. For how foolish that idolizing of others turns out to be most of the time, because no one but you is ever God. Help me to see others as they really are—as children of God, like me, but not themselves God. And help me to laugh at myself when I try to make others into images of what only you alone can be—all holy, all powerful, all good, Lord.

OF THE
PORTIUNCULA INDULGENCE

ARLY one morning Francis and I, Brother Masseo, left the Portiuncula and walked to the city of Perugia, where the Papal court was then residing. We were on a very unusual mission, for Francis was going to ask Pope Honorius III, the successor of Pope Innocent III, for a favor unheard of at that time.

When we arrived, we were immediately admitted into the presence of the Lord Pope. And Francis said, "Most Holy Father, there is a little Benedictine chapel on the plain below Assisi. It is rightly called the Portiuncula, the Little Portion, because it is the little portion of this earth that the Lord has lent us where we might live out the Rule of Life you approved for us."

"Yes?"

"Well, Most Holy Father, I humbly ask a special indulgence for this little church so that anyone who prays there on the anniversary of its consecration may receive the indulgence with no offering of any kind being made."

"Brother Francis, I do not think it would be right to grant an indulgence without requiring the person to do something. But what kind of indulgence do you want? One year? Three years?"

But Francis said, "Oh, Holy Father, what is a mere three years compared to eternity?"

"Then what are you asking for, Brother Francis?"

"Holy Father, I am asking for souls, not years."

"And what does that mean?"

"It means, Holy Father, that I am asking for everyone who enters the Portiuncula, after having confessed their sins and having received absolution, that they be freed of the guilt and punishment for all the sins they have committed from the day of their baptism to that very moment of entering the church."

"You are asking for more than is the custom of the Holy See to grant."

"But, Holy Father, it is not Francis who asks but the Lord Jesus Christ, who sent me to you."

Then the Holy Father, who knew Francis' holiness and closeness to the Lord, said in the presence of the Papal court, "Then I will grant your request."

And he repeated this statement three times, adding "In the name of the Lord. So be it."

But the cardinals immediately objected, saying "But this will undermine the Crusades and the pilgrimage to Rome, Holy Father. For who would go forth to do battle with the Saracens in the Holy Land or brave the dangerous journey to Rome if they can gain the same indulgence by doing nothing but going to Umbria?"

"I will not revoke what I have granted," Pope Honorius answered. "I have done it. It cannot be reversed."

"But then reduce the indulgence, at least."

And the Lord Pope Honorius turned again to Francis and said, "Brother Francis, this plenary indulgence is given for all time, but only for one day of the year, the day of the dedication of this little church, from first vespers of the day before to vespers of August 2, including the whole night."

Then Francis and I bowed our heads and with great joy turned to leave the palace. But Pope Honorius called us back, saying "Where are you going, dear brothers? You have no proof of this indulgence. Wait till the secretary is finished drafting the papers."

But Francis said, "Most Holy Father, your word is enough for us. If this indulgence is God's will, God will make it known. We have no need of documents, for the Virgin Mary is the parchment, Christ the notary, and the angels are our witnesses."

And, indeed, the Holy Father's word was enough, for this indulgence drew penitents from near and far, though Pope Honorius put no word to paper. ✤

In 1921 the Holy See granted the Portiuncula Indulgence exactly as St. Francis wanted it—namely, a plenary indulgence valid every day of the year for those who visit the Portiuncula, are free from sin and have recently received the Eucharist, and pray for the intentions of the Pope. But since 1967 this same privilege is obtainable at every church. And though present church practice does not emphasize the granting of indulgences, especially those attached to a particular place rather than to the practice of virtue, thousands of pilgrims still flock to Assisi on the day of the Portiuncula Pardon, some crawling on their knees through the large basilica to the Portiuncula chapel, which rests under the central dome.

There is a hymn attributed to Brother Leo that sums up what has happened to these pilgrims throughout the ages:

Hic fuit arctata	Here the old way's
veteris via lata,	broad highway has
et dilatata	changed into life
virtus in gente vocata.	eternal's narrow way;
	and virtue is freely
	given to people called
	from every nation.

ST. FRANCIS AND THE SULTAN

HEN one rules, one learns to respect power. My armies were triumphing across Egypt bringing me great wealth and acquisitions of land. War, killing—these are in my blood, my nature. I killed for my god Allah just as the Pope killed for his god, this Christ. And nowhere was this more evident than between Christians and Saracens in the Holy Land. Both of us were determined to seize the Holy Places, one for Allah and the other for Christ, as if God himself could be divided up according to how he was understood and interpreted by his different prophets. And so great was the division between Saracen and Christian that neither felt safe and vindicated unless his enemy was killed or utterly conquered. And so it went: The Holy Land for Allah! The Holy Land for Christ! And all the while our followers were perishing daily, falling in battle at the hands of the other.

It was to this terrible scene that a ragged holy man called Francis came to preach to me. He carried no sword. At first, I thought he was a fool, a coward; but then I realized his courage was in his faith. In simplicity and poverty of spirit, Francis came into my very camp, where he was bound and tortured. Then he was brought before me so I could seal his fate, but out of curiosity, I ordered this stranger to speak.

"I know your kind, holy beggar. You want to be a martyr, don't you?"

"Yes," Francis said. "And I want to suffer martyrdom for the love of my Lord Jesus Christ, who . . ."

"Yes, and now I get the sermon. I am not interested in preaching, holy man, nor in martyrdom. I am a sultan, I prefer signs and wonders. You do have some of those up your sleeve, don't you?"

"Yes and no, great leader." Francis seemed to be unaccountably warming up to me.

"Yes and no?"

"Well, I have no magic, if that is what you mean. But I have faith, faith in Jesus Christ, which will enable me to stand the test."

"And what test is that, holy man?"

"The test of all those who love God, the test of fire."

There was a murmur among my sages, as Francis went on.

"Let us light a big fire here, and I will enter the fire with your sages, and God will show us which faith is more sure, more holy."

But I, noticing out of the corner of my eye one of my priests, an old, esteemed man, slipping away, replied, "I am a superstitious man, but I have never cared for priests and their potions and incantations. They hide behind their robes and whimper. I like men with swords and horses. What would I care if one of these priests were burned in a fire? But you at least have courage and do seem willing to stand behind your words."

"Well, then, great Sultan, would you and your people embrace the Christian religion if I entered the fire alone and emerged unharmed?"

"And are you that sure, holy man?"

"No, great Sultan. But I know that if I am burned in the fire, it will be because I am a sinner and you will attribute it to my sin of presumption. However, if I am not burned, it will be because of the power of God, and you will attribute my being saved to Christ, the true God, the Lord and Savior of all."

It was an interesting proposal, but I had to decline. "That challenge I cannot accept, holy man, for it would cause a riot among my people."

Nevertheless, I had come to respect this barefoot man before me, and so I offered Francis gifts of friendship, which he acknowledged but politely refused. I then provided him safe passage from my camp.

Before he left, Francis said, "Sire, I shall indeed leave and return home, but when I go to heaven at God's call, I tell you now that I will send you two of my brothers and from them you will receive baptism in the name of Jesus Christ and be saved."

And so it came to pass. For when I lay in my final illness, I remembered Francis' words and found myself waiting for them to come true.

Thereupon, two of Francis' brothers came into the land and asked safe passage to see me. And as I had been waiting for them, I sent for them immediately. They, in turn, told me that St. Francis had appeared to them from heaven and sent them to bring salvation to his friend, the Sultan. And so it was that I believed. ✦

St. Francis' whole life in Christ was a making of peace, after having been a maker of war as a young man. He made peace among the factions in Assisi, between towns, between people and wild animals, between sultans and kings. His *Canticle of the Creatures* is itself a song of praise and reconciliation.

But the prayer of reconciliation most people 'associate with St. Francis is: "Make Me an Instrument of Your Peace." Unfortunately this prayer can only be found in twentieth-century sources and is therefore not an authentic prayer of St. Francis. It does, however, express most poignantly who St. Francis was and how he lived. It is indeed a Franciscan Peace Prayer.

Lord, make me an instrument of your peace.
Where there is hatred, let me sow love;
Where there is injury, pardon;
Where there is doubt, faith;
Where there is despair, hope;
Where there is darkness, light;
And where there is sadness, joy.

O Divine Master,
Grant that I may not so much seek to be consoled as to
console,
To be understood as to understand,
To be loved as to love;
For it is in giving that we receive;
It is in pardoning that we are pardoned
And it is in dying that we are born to eternal life.

THE DAMIETTA PROSTITUTE

HEN I was a young woman, Francis came with the Crusaders to Damietta in Egypt. He did not wage war or bear arms. Instead, he spoke of peace and a man called Jesus Christ, whom he was determined to talk about to the Sultan himself. And I think the Sultan was greatly moved by Francis and his story—more, by his courage. And though Francis failed to bring peace between the Crusaders and the Saracens, he did work a marvelous conversion in at least one single heart, mine.

One evening as Francis and one of his brothers were

walking cold and weary along the road, they saw an inn and decided to stop and rest there overnight.

Now while they sat at table eating, I approached Francis and invited him to join me in one of the rooms. And Francis, much to the amazement of his companion, readily agreed, saying "Yes, but if you want me to do what you want, you must also do what I want."

"I agree," I replied. "Let us go then, and prepare a bed."

So he followed me to a room where there was a large bed and a fireplace whose flames lit up the room. I was about to lead him to the bed when he stopped me and, stripping himself naked, said, "Before I join you in your bed, come, join me in mine." Thereupon he went to the blazing fireplace and lay down in the flames upon the iron grate.

Then Francis called to me, "Quickly now, undress and join me in this wonderful bed of flowers, for you agreed to do whatever I wanted."

But I was moved with fear. Was this holy man a sorcerer? He was not burned, and in fact continued to beckon me to lie down with him in the fire as though in flowers. This little man filled me with wonder and love as he smiled gently, praising God. And I knew at once what manner of fire this was. And I knelt down upon the floor and surrendered my soul to the purifying flames. I asked God to forgive my sins and those of all the men I'd lain with, and immediately I felt through my whole being the healing touch of God's mercy and love.

Then, like Mary Magdalene, in the Gospel, I gave myself wholly to the Lord Jesus, and He won many souls through me in all the region of Damietta. ❧

AFTER HIS CONVERSION St. Francis called his body "Brother Ass." And though he fasted and deprived his physical self into poor health, he later repented of this harshness and asked Brother Ass to forgive him. Our bodies are as much a part of God's creation as our souls. They require care, protection, respect. They give us pleasure, and it is through them that we embrace others. The beauty of the "embrace" between Francis and the prostitute is that he showed her a way to see herself as truly beautiful, aflame with a heavenly countenance. He spoke to her in the language she would understand, body to body, flesh to flesh.

Lord, let me be a witness to true love, as St. Francis was to the Damietta prostitute and you were to Mary Magdalene and the woman caught in adultery. Let me not be self-righteous and pious, so that I drive away those whom you ate with when you were on earth. Let me be as merciful and loving to others as you are to me. Teach me the language of real love.

St. Francis and
Brother Leo Try to Pray

ARLY on in the Order, Francis and I had no books to say the office by. So at midnight when the hour of matins came, Francis said to me, "Dear son, we have no breviaries to pray matins by; so in order that we may still spend this time in praising God, I will speak and you answer as I instruct you; and be careful not to change the words in any way. I shall say something like 'O Brother Francis, you have committed so many sins and evils in this world that you really are deserving of hell'; and then, Brother Leo, you answer, 'How true. In fact, you deserve the lowest depth of hell.'" I knew Francis well enough by then to humor him, so I agreed, saying "Anything you say, father; I am ready, in the name of God."

Then Francis began to lament: "O Brother Francis, you have committed so many sins and evils in the world that you are deserving of hell." Then, in spite of myself, I answered, "God will work so much good through you that you will go to Paradise." But Francis objected, saying "No, Brother Leo, that is not it. Rather, when I say, 'Brother Francis, you have worked so much iniquity against God that you are worthy of His curse,' you say, 'I agree totally. You *are* worthy to be numbered among the damned.'" "Right," I said. "Now I've got it."

So once again Francis cried aloud with tears and sighs

and beating of his breast, "O my Lord of heaven and earth, I have wrought so much iniquity, I have sinned so often against you that I am altogether deserving to be damned by you." But try as I might, I could only answer, "O Brother Francis, God will work in you so powerfully that among the blessed you will be most blessed."

Then Francis, surprised that I had again disobeyed him, reproved me, saying "Why aren't you following my instructions? I command you now by holy obedience to answer me exactly as I tell you to. I shall begin like this: 'O wretched and vile Brother Francis, do you now presume upon God's mercy, when you have committed so many sins against the Father of mercy and the God of all consolation? You are not worthy of finding His mercy.' And then, Brother Leo, little lamb, you answer, 'That is certain. You are in no way worthy of finding God's mercy.' " But when Francis said, "O wretched and vile Brother Francis," and all the rest, I again answered, "God the Father, whose mercy is infinitely greater than your sin, will show you great mercy, and what's more, will pour upon you many graces."

At this reply, Francis demanded of me, "And now, after repeatedly contradicting me, do you even have the boldness to violate holy obedience?" But I could only humbly and reverently reply, "God knows, my father, that each time you spoke I had every intention of answering as you commanded; but God made me speak as it pleased Him, not as I wanted to." And at that Francis was filled with wonder and said to me, "I pray you most lovingly, my brother, that this time you answer me just as I instructed."

And I said, "Then speak in the name of God, and this time I will indeed answer as you wish."

And Francis, weeping afresh, said, "O Brother Francis, wretched and vile one, do you really think that God will have mercy on you?" But out of my mouth came, "Yes, and you shall receive great grace from God, and He shall exalt and glorify you forever, for every one who humbles self shall be exalted . . . and, no, I cannot say anything else, since it is God who is speaking through my mouth." And so it continued, this humble strife, with many tears and much spiritual consolation, Francis and I keeping watch until dawn. ❧

THIS STRANGE TALE of Francis and Brother Leo has much to say to us of the importance of having a friend who will tell us the truth about ourselves. If we are too much alone, too isolated from others, it is easy to have warped views about ourselves, thinking we are better, or more often, worse than we really are.

From the very beginning of the Order, St. Francis stressed the importance of fraternity, of having brothers and sisters to tell one's story to. Each year at the General Chapter, Francis and his brothers would come together to tell their stories of what happened on the road, to confess their sins to one another, and to receive absolution from those brothers who were priests. So important was this fraternity, this sharing, that St. Francis considered the brotherhood itself the only home of the brothers. Since they owned no houses, their very interrelating was their home.

Lord, give me such a home, and people it with your graces.

ON DISCERNING GOD'S WILL

S more and more men joined, Francis began to wonder about the direction the Order was taking, and specifically about his own direction. The call to prayer was so deep within him that he began to question the intensely active life he was living. Should he perhaps withdraw completely from others and give himself to prayer and contemplation in the solitude of a mountain?

He was not sure; thus, as was his custom, he sought the counsel of others so that he would not be deceived by the intensity of his own selfish desires. Francis therefore sent for me and said, "Brother Masseo, go first to the Lady Clare and then to Brother Sylvester in order that through them I might know what the Lord wants me to do."

Brother Sylvester, who was the same priest who had joined the Order through the example of Brother Bernard's giving away all his money, was living in intense prayer and contemplation on Mount Subasio. And when Sylvester heard my request, he turned immediately to the

Lord for advice and counsel. And when he returned, these are the words Brother Sylvester gave me from the Lord: "Brother Francis, the Lord says that he has not called you to this state only for yourself, but that you may reap a harvest of souls and that many souls may be saved through your preaching and your example."

Then I went back to Lady Clare to learn what answer she had received in prayer. And she said that she and the companion with whom she had prayed had received the same words from God as I reported to them from Brother Sylvester. So with that I returned to Francis, who received me like an emissary from the Great King. He knelt down and washed my feet and then prepared a meal for me. And when we had eaten, Francis led me into the silence of the woods, where he knelt down before me on the ground. Then he bared his head and crossed his arms and asked in a hushed prayerlike voice, "What is it, then, dear brother, that my Lord Jesus Christ commands me to do?"

And I reported that the Lord had answered the prayers of Brother Sylvester and the Lady Clare and her companion, and he had revealed to all three the same command: "That he wants you, Father Francis to continue going about the world preaching, because he has not called you for yourself only, but for the salvation of others."

He sprang to his feet and embraced me, saying "Then, my brother, what are we doing here? Let us now take to the road as the Lord has shown us!"

MEDIEVAL THEOLOGIANS defined devotion as an alacrity, an eagerness in doing the will of God. The devout person hears the word of God and immediately puts it into practice. Devotion, then, is almost a definition of St. Francis' life. From the very beginning, he was a man of action. He listened, and he carried out what he heard.

True devotion demands fulfilling God's will. Either we do what God asks of us or we don't. For us, discerning God's will is frequently much less direct than some of the messages and visions Francis received. But we can all use this particular example of asking others to pray and hearing their answers and solutions to our questions. Lord, forgive me; so many times I have been unwilling to hear any other than my own thoughts and ideas, busy knowing what is best for me, without even asking you.

BROTHER JUNIPER AND
BROTHER JOHN THE SIMPLE

 WAS to the Francisan court a jester and fool of whom Father Francis once said, "If only I had a whole forest of such junipers!" Mine was the wisdom of Masseo stripped down to its most primitive, unadorned form. In me there was no comeliness, no imposing figure like Masseo's. In me there was the raw holiness of one who only looked at God and did not see the consternation his bizarre antics was causing, as I sought to please only the Lord of Heaven.

I cared nothing for human wisdom and caution and prudence; I had let it all go years earlier when I fell in love with God. Nor did I change when I joined the Order. I simply remained who I was. And I was not so simple as I seemed. My simplicity was well intended to mask the powerful work of God in my life.

But to really understand the kind of man I was, you have to know the story of another brother, the one we call John the Simple. This John was a farmer, a man who had walked behind a team of oxen all his life, never complaining, faithfully working to support his aging parents and his younger sisters.

One day when Francis passed through his region, the farmer, John, who had heard much of the great penitent from Assisi, sought Francis out. He revealed to Francis what no one had ever suspected of this seemingly contented farmer who appeared destined, like his ancestors before him, to work the soil, to follow the pull of the oxen, to marry and have children and be laid to rest in the very soil made fruitful and rich by his labors.

What a surprise it was to everyone around, when this seemingly unthinking man returned from his conversation with Francis and unhitched one of the oxen and brought it to him. It was all he had of his inheritance, his only possession to give away before joining Francis and his brothers as a Lesser Brother of Penance.

His parents and sisters began to wail and wring their hands, and they came running to Francis and their brother John because they were very poor and their own brother had just reduced them to destitution by presuming to take as his own one of the oxen they needed to till the land. They all began to talk at once and to gesticulate with great sweeping movements of their arms and hands as if Francis were too great and noble to understand their poor words.

But Francis calmed them with the sign of the cross and assured them they could have the ox. Their brother's intention had been good, for to become a Lesser Brother one must give one's all to the poor. However, since he had nothing of his own to give, their brother had presumed to take one oxen as being justly his for all the work he had done to keep the family alive. Now, whether the ox was his or not, these people were no doubt among the poorest of the poor, so who better to give it to than to his own family?

And his family, when they heard the last sentence, began to rejoice, but only briefly, for now they realized they were losing him who alone knew the oxen. Their son and broth er's whole life had been to know best how to make the oxen walk straight rows and preserve their strength and keep the pace even and unhurried, that they might live long, productive lives. Now they were losing him without whom the oxen were only animals to feed and care for, a further drain upon the family's meager resources. And they began to wail aloud once more.

Francis, however, assured them that God himself had summoned the man of the family off the land he had worked so long. And God would surely see that they would do right well if they gladly let him go into the service of God, who alone could make the wheat and grasses grow.

John's parents said it was easy for Francis to say that, because he didn't have to work the fields when he was too old or a frail young girl, but they agreed that no one dare oppose the call of God. And so they went back to their home reluctantly, trying to have faith, prodding the reluctant ox away from him who had understood the way it is with oxen.

And so Brother John became one of the Lesser Brothers; and as it was with Francis himself, nothing further is known of his parents and how they fared without their son. Faith says they received a hundredfold for such a sacrifice.

Be that as it may, their son was now so grateful to Francis and so eager to imitate him, that he began to ape every act and gesture of the saint. If Francis would spit or cough, Brother John would do the same. Or if Francis would begin to pray or weep over the Passion of Jesus, so would Brother John, until finally Francis had to gently reprimand him and explain to him that he must not imitate him but, rather, walk as his own man in the footsteps of his Lord Jesus Christ. Just as John had followed behind the oxen and had come to know and understand their every movement, so now he must follow in the footsteps of his Lord, letting *him* lead, coming to know every signal he gave along the way.

Brother John was very grateful for these words and asked forgiveness for being so simple as to follow the wrong ox. And he thanked Francis for making everything so clear. Now he would not need to imitate, which, he admitted, had been very hard for him because he did not know how to do anything but follow. And follow is what Brother John did from then on. He followed in the footsteps of Jesus without swerving from his row and so became known as John the Simple, the Lesser Brother who knew best what Jesus meant when he said, "My yoke is easy and my burden light." He knew well his Lord, and oxen, and other beasts of burden. ❧

LORD, AS ST. FRANCIS did not imitate you but followed in your footsteps, teach me not to imitate St. Francis or any of your saints, but to follow in their footsteps following you. They must become transparent that I might see you. It is your footsteps that they lead me to, and they are useful only when my foot rests in their footprint resting in yours. You alone, Lord, lead us to the Father.

Brother Juniper and the Farmer's Pig

LL OF this about Brother John the Simple leads to me, Brother Juniper, who, not knowing the way it is with animals, cut off the foot of a pig! And saying that I did not know how it is with animals, really means that I paid no heed to them, as Blessed Francis did to every creature. So bent was I on doing one thing at a time, so intent and single-minded was I in my simplicity, that I would often do unconscionable things in my zeal to please God. And then Francis would have to reprimand me, as he did Brother John, for my misguided zeal.

It is true that I did grow somewhat in wisdom, but at the beginning I was truly more simple than wise, and because of that flaw, I used to do unthinking, even cruel things in my desire to love God and my brothers. And that is why I did so awful a thing as the following tale relates.

There was at that time among us brothers a great love and concern for one another, so that we were quite keen to tend to one another's needs as soon as those needs became evident. We lived in deep and quiet prayer like Mary of Bethany, but as soon as one of us became troubled or ill, we would busy ourselves like Martha and try to outdo one another in charity.

And so it came to pass that I was once visiting a sick brother at St. Mary of the Angels; and when I saw how much the brother was suffering, I was moved with compassion and asked if there was anything I could do. Was there something the sick brother would like to eat that might strengthen him? And the brother's eyes lit up, and he said eagerly, "Oh yes, Brother Juniper! If only I could have a succulent morsel of pig's foot such as my mother used to prepare for us when we were sick!"

No sooner were these words out of the sick friar's mouth than I was running out of the cell, calling back to the brother that I would be back with the finest pig's foot he had eaten since he was a boy. But instead of going to the market and begging the pig's foot, I ran straight toward a group of pigs who were feeding in the fields. Then, with a knife I had snatched from the kitchen as I left the friary, I cut off the foot of a startled little pig that I had wrestled to the ground with great difficulty.

Leaving the poor little pig screaming in great pain, deaf to its cries, I ran off merrily to prepare the pig's foot for the sick brother. But how often an inordinate zeal makes us blind and deaf to the pain we are causing others. So, as I ran blithely on my way to minister to my brother, the poor little pig lay bleeding to death and squealing, and the farmer came running to see what was wrong with his pig.

When I arrived at the Portiuncula, I served up the pig's foot, and the sick brother ate it with great relish, much to my delight. But just as the brother was finishing the last of the delicious morsel, there was a great clamor outside. It was the farmer screaming and cursing us friars, for the man tending his pigs had seen what I had done and dutifully reported it to his master.

The commotion was so great that Francis was shaken

from his prayer and came out to see what the matter was. And when he heard what had happened, he apologized for his brothers and promised to make good the farmer's loss. But the man would not be appeased; he continued to heap curses on us, and then he turned his back and walked away in a rage.

Then Francis turned to ask us who it was who had done such a terrible thing. But before he could ask, his eyes fell upon me, and he knew it could only have been me. And so he dismissed the other brothers and asked me, "Brother, was it you who cut off the foot of our Brother Pig?"

"Oh, yes, Father Francis!" And then with gusto I told the story of the sick brother's need and how I, even little I, was able to help the brother so easily.

And when I finished my account, it was difficult for Francis, in the face of such enthusiasm, to reprimand me; but justice and the need to instruct in the true way of Jesus made Francis firm.

"Oh, Brother Juniper, through ignorance and blind zeal you have done a great injustice to this poor farmer, and you have caused pain and maybe even death to one of God's dear creatures, our little Brother Pig. You must hasten now and throw yourself at the farmer's feet and beg his forgiveness; and on your way, beg God's forgiveness, too, for what you have done to Brother Pig, who even now may be bleeding to death. And promise the farmer to right the damage, too, because you have surely ruined our good name as well as stealing and harming the word of God!"

But I could only stand there in disbelief that anyone, especially my holy Father Francis, could be angry when all I had tried to do was practice the charity commanded by Christ in the Gospel. For I was still very much a man of my times wherein pigbaiting and cruel games involving animals were looked upon simply as diversion and sport and of no consequence to human beings.

But I was always obedient and was about to rush off to right the wrong Father Francis insisted I had done, when the last of Francis' words reached my heart and I did not know what they meant, that I must make amends for "harming the word of God!" I wanted to stop and ask the holy Father to explain these strange and terrifying words to me, but I knew that obedience always comes first and usually answers the very question we are tempted to postpone obedience for, in our haste to find its answer.

I came to the farmer and fell at his feet, telling him that his pig had been the cause of a great work of charity for a sick little brother of God. But the farmer would not hear of it and became even more angry, heaping much abuse upon me and coming almost to the point of striking me. But in my simplicity, I only thought the man had not understood my poor speech, so I began again to tell the story of what had happened, this time kneeling on the ground, my eyes raised to heaven, as if I were reciting a story from Holy Writ.

Then the farmer, at the end of his patience, was about to start screaming and pulling at his hair, when suddenly he realized how truly simple was this man he thought was merely a liar or at least a fool of the worst kind. And he began to listen and be moved by the sincerity of my reason for cutting off the foot of his pig. And the farmer then began to weep for his own possessiveness and lack of charity. He realized that he had never made a gift of one of his pigs to anyone, never given of what the Lord had freely given him, for I was just then crying out with great unction that everything we have is only lent to us by our Father, the great Almsgiver, and we should be willing to give freely of God's gifts to our fellow human beings.

And the farmer, with great remorse, knelt down beside me and asked my forgiveness for his selfishness. Then he embraced me and lifted me up from the ground and hurried me off to the field of pigs. There he had the poor, suffering pig slaughtered and well dressed and cooked; and he and I ceremoniously carried the roasted pig to Francis and the other brothers. Then, with joyful hearts, we all sat down together at table and ate.

But while we were feasting and celebrating God's gifts and the reconciliation that had taken place, Blessed Francis suddenly stood up and began to speak as if in ecstasy: "My brothers, you have gone from bad to worse. First you harmed God's word and then you killed it. Be careful to eat of this pig with great reverence as if it were the Body of the Lord, for every creature is a word spoken by God. And it is only by God's leave that we dare partake of what his word has created. We must, therefore, never kill one of God's creatures, not even to nourish ourselves, without first asking permission of him whose word the creature is."

And then I knew how it was that I had harmed the word of God and even more stupidly had killed it. And I fell to my knees, begging God's pardon and promising never again to harm any of God's little words. ❧

WHAT BROTHER JUNIPER DOES in this story must surely seem a terrible thing to most people. And yet, who of us does not have compulsions that lead to similar indiscretions and even to cruelty, thoughtlessness and injustice? And add to that the zeal for God and neighbor that has led to more than the cutting of a pig's foot. We have killed one another and destroyed nations and even whole peoples and subjugated others, all with an earnestness like Brother Juniper's.

Only reverence for everything that is can remedy blind fervor. And only humble listening to each person, each thing, for the word of God it speaks, will make me reverent. Otherwise, I use and manipulate and twist everything to my own purposes and compulsions, disguised as love of God and neighbor.

Lord, open my whole being to what each creature is asking of me before I demand something of it.

How Brother Juniper
Seesawed with Children

ONCE Brother Juniper was on his way to Rome when a large number of us who were his admirers heard he was coming and went out to meet him. But Brother Juniper saw us coming and started looking for a way to escape our fawning praise of his holiness. He recognized at once that we were looking for someone holy to affirm us in our holier-than-thou posture, so off he ran toward a boy and girl who were teeter-tottering nearby. They had put one log across another and were gleefully seesawing up and down.

Brother Juniper ran over to the children and asked, loud enough for us to hear, "Can I play too?"

The little girl laughingly gave up her place to him, and he lifted her off the log and sat down opposite the boy and began seesawing as enthusiastically as a child. The children loved his performance, and none of them paid the least attention to us when we came up to them and watched in embarrassment and chagrin as our "saint" made a fool of himself on our behalf.

As Brother Juniper just kept seesawing with the boy and waving happily to the little girl as if we were not there, it was obvious that he was purposely ignoring us. But we tried to put a good face on it all, saying "Isn't he wonderful with little children?"

However, when Brother Juniper continued to pay no attention to us, some of our group became angry and stomped off, grumbling "What kind of a fool is this? And who does he think he is to look down his infantile nose at us and dismiss us as nobodies?"

But some of us, though we didn't like it, did understand what he was doing and let him alone. We went away sad, though, because we realized that we had forgotten how to play. In our silly search for someone "holy" to associate with, someone who would sympathize with our own self-righteous piety, we had missed those who were really holy. ✢

LORD, HOW GREAT IS the temptation to do good works or pray in public in order to be seen and admired by others. And yet, you tell us that when we pray, we should go into our closet and pray to our Father in secret as you did. And you remind us not to parade our works before others in order to be seen and honored. For our Father, who sees and hears in secret, will also reward us in secret.

Lord, help me to be more like Brother Juniper, who never took himself or others so seriously that he could no longer laugh at himself and other human beings. Help me, like him, to take no one, including myself, as seriously as I take you.

How Brother Rufino Preached

I BROTHER Rufino, am the cousin of St. Clare and a member of the noble house of Offreduccio. And though I am noble, I had first to become a fool in the world's eyes and lose my dignity before a spiritual dignity could ever truly be mine. And the holy Father Francis knew this well from the experience of his own fall from honor and respect in the eyes of the citizens of Assisi.

And that is why Francis asked me to undertake something exceedingly bitter for me, shy and quiet as I was. For even though I carried myself with all the dignity of my background, I found it very hard to speak in public. I would begin to tremble and stammer and lower my eyes and end up silent and confused and ashamed.

Just the same, though he knew my fear, Francis once said to me, "Dearest Brother Rufino, it is God's will that you go into the city and preach the Gospel to all the people. And see to it, dear brother, that you first go through the streets naked except for your undergarments."

Well, you can imagine the effect these words had upon me. I stood before Francis in utter disbelief, but seeing the total seriousness and sincerity in Francis' eyes, I then and there stripped myself of my habit and went off into the city where my family was held in great esteem. And as I passed into the Piazza del Comune, a shocked group of citizens gathered around me.

"Surely all this penance and fasting is driving these followers of Bernardone's son completely mad!" one old man yelled.

"This can't be Rufino of the Offreduccio!" said another.

Then, one after another, people began to voice their disdain, which led to abuse, which led to a cruel and derisive laughter.

Meanwhile, I had begun to make my way into one of the churches, where I mounted the pulpit and began to preach as well as I could to the unruly crowd that had followed me in. All I could do was repeat over and over again, like a small child who has just learned a nursery rhyme, "Leave the world, give up sin. Give back to others what is rightly theirs or you will perish. Keep the commandments and love God and your neighbors. And you will have life everlasting. Therefore, repent, for the Kingdom of Heaven is drawing near."

Over and over, I said it until my stammer began to sound like a singsong rhyme. Then, just as I thought I would surely faint amid their uproarious laughter, who should come through the open doors in his undergarments and join me in the pulpit but Francis himself!

The crowd was so startled that they stopped in midlaughter as if their mouths were frozen open, locked by some cramp of their jaws' hinges. And looking around, they saw Brother Leo standing in the open doorway, and draped over his arms like banners were two habits, mine and that of the Blessed Francis.

At the sight of two nearly naked men standing in the pulpit, one the son of a nobleman, the other the son of a rich merchant, the people were at first silent, as in the moment before some momentous announcement. And then the tension was too much for them, and they were pushed over the edge of awe and surprise, and they began laughing uncontrollably right there in church, some of them doubling over and others rolling on the floor like children without inhibitions.

But Francis only smiled at me and apologized for asking me to do something so hard without going with me so that we might experience shame together as brothers.

"Forgive me, dear brother," he said. "I have laid upon you a heavy burden which I was not willing to share with you, though I did so unthinkingly and not out of malice."

And Francis then embraced me and, turning to the scene of mayhem below, began to preach so full of unction over the nakedness of the Lord Jesus Christ crucified that a profound change began to fall over the crowd. As Francis drew the picture of our Savior's nakedness and shame upon the cross their laughter turned to tears, and quiet weeping was heard throughout the church and out into the piazza. Brother Leo stood like a squire rapt by the words of his knight.

Many of Assisi's citizens were converted to Jesus Christ that day, and to my surprise, many of them said it was not the preaching of Francis that moved them. As one prominent citizen was heard to say, "It was Brother Rufino who moved me, for he suffered shame for Christ and spoke to us, though he shook and stammered. And when the son of Bernardone ascended the pulpit, Rufino, though a nobleman, yielded and let Francis speak. Because of his humility I was moved to tears by the image of the poor, naked

Christ that Brother Rufino became as Francis continued to
preach." ✦

I<small>T IS SAID THAT</small> St. John-Baptist Vianney was so frightened
of preaching that he read his sermons holding the pages in
front of his face so that he could neither see nor be seen by
the congregation. And yet, as he trembled and continued
to read, people would experience profound conversions.

How much good you could do through me, Lord, if only
I could muster the courage to risk making a fool of myself
for you. If only I were less self-conscious and more conscious, more focused on you. If only I could trust your
words that what I am to say "will be given" me "when the
time comes" and that it will not be I who speak but the
spirit of "my father" (Mt 10:19–20).

Lord, give me courage to trust your gifts in me, despite
my awkwardness with them.

How Brother Stephen
Was Cured

I WAS one of the brothers who was received into the Order by Blessed Francis himself, but I was not happy and at peace like the others. I was afflicted with frenzied outbursts and was deeply disturbed in mind and heart. No one knew what my affliction was, and many said I was possessed by an evil spirit. Finally, I could no longer bear it and went in earnest to Father Francis for help, but the Holy Father sent me instead to the Lady Clare. He did not explain why, but only said that in her touch I would find healing.

Now, the Lady Clare, in obedience to Father Francis, gladly received me, even though when she opened the door, I began to shake and scream. She simply made the sign of the cross upon my forehead, telling me to retire and sleep in the place where she was accustomed to pray.

I willingly received the cross traced upon my forehead and went to the Lady Clare's place in the choir. There I fell into a deep sleep. And when I awoke, I was completely cured of my madness, and I returned to Francis.

That is all I know, except that now I am happy and at peace like the others. ❧

LORD, I PRAY FOR YOUR healing touch through your holy ones. For you purify their touch by the sign of your cross, which they offer me as a healing. I pray, Lord, that I can embrace the cross that is your touch, for in that embrace is the quieting, the sleep that evades me when I refuse to relinquish control and let you be the power of healing within.

HOW SATAN DECEIVED BROTHER RUFINO

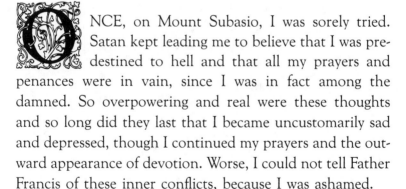 NCE, on Mount Subasio, I was sorely tried. Satan kept leading me to believe that I was predestined to hell and that all my prayers and penances were in vain, since I was in fact among the damned. So overpowering and real were these thoughts and so long did they last that I became uncustomarily sad and depressed, though I continued my prayers and the outward appearance of devotion. Worse, I could not tell Father Francis of these inner conflicts, because I was ashamed.

Then, to add to my confusion and growing despair, Satan appeared to me as the Crucified Savior and said, "Oh,

Brother Rufino, why are you praying like this, so earnest and bathed in tears? Don't you know you are among the damned? And don't listen anymore to the Blessed Francis, for he, like his father, is also predestined to hell. He is deceiving you if he says you are good, for who would know better than I who is condemned?"

Then Satan departed and I fell into an even deeper despair, losing even my faith in Blessed Francis. I withdrew further into myself and refused to approach Francis and the other brothers.

But God revealed to Francis what was happening to me in my cave of despair, and he sent Brother Masseo to bring me to him.

When Brother Masseo approached my cave and told me Francis wanted to talk with me, I haughtily said, "What do I have to do with that deceiver? Don't you know he is among those condemned to hell?"

And Brother Masseo replied, "Oh, my brother, you have certainly been deceived by the Evil One. Our Father Francis is a good man and brings blessings and peace on us all." And with these and other words he convinced me to go with him.

Then Francis saw me from afar, and he came out to meet me, saying "Dear brother, why are you so sad? Whom have you been listening to, good and holy Brother Rufino?"

Then I began to weep and stammer the whole story to Blessed Francis. And when I finished, Francis said to me, "My dearest Brother Rufino, nobleman of Assisi and of the Kingdom, it is not Christ Crucified whom you have seen, but Satan in his guise. For the dear Christ always brings peace, not despair. Therefore, the next time Satan comes to you in this guise, say to him, 'Open your mouth one more time and I'll defecate in it.' At that, I assure you, the Evil One will flee and your peace of soul and body will be restored."

And so it happened. For as I began to pray with tears of joy because of the peace Blessed Francis' words had brought me, the Crucified again appeared to me and said, "What is this, Brother Rufino? Still praying, even though you know for certain that you are damned?"

Then I repeated the words Blessed Francis had told me to say, and the Devil, unmasked, departed with a great clamor and an avalanche of stones that brought Francis and the other brothers from their caves to see what was happening. Then I emerged from my cave and told them the whole story, and we all broke into praise.

I then returned to prayer with renewed tears of joy, and Christ Jesus himself appeared to me and said, "You did well, my son, to listen to Brother Francis and believe him, for he who tormented you was indeed the Devil. I am your Lord, Jesus Christ, and as a sign to you, I say to you that as long as you are on this mountain, you will never again be sad or depressed."

And so it was, for when the Blessed Christ left me, I remained rapt in prayer night and day, and so full of grace, blessing, and the certainty of eternal life that I would have remained the rest of my life on Mount Subasio, had I not learned my lesson well that there is more peace and certitude in simple obedience and faith in one's spiritual guide than in visions and ecstasy.

Later, when Blessed Francis told us we were leaving the mountain, I too left gladly and willingly and was not a little surprised on the way down the mountain when Francis said, "Brothers, there is now a saint among us. For Brother Rufino, nobleman of Assisi and kinsman of the Lady Clare, has been canonized in heaven by the Lord Jesus Christ himself, even while he is still alive and with us. Praised be the Lord Jesus Christ." ❧

WHAT FRANCIS WAS SAYING to Rufino was that if something does not bring you peace, then it is not from God—even if it appears to be God sent.

We must discern in our hearts what things, which images and dreams are from God. Sometimes we think we are no good, or destined for hell, or unforgivable. Sometimes we think that the Evil One has us in his grip or even that there is no Evil One, no Eternity, no God.

Lord God, all of these thoughts, fears, lack of faith and understanding come from our hearts, not from yours. For you have said so clearly that before the world was made, you chose us.

"I chose you in my Son Jesus Christ, to be holy and faultless, and to live through love in my presence. I determined that you should become my adopted child through Jesus Christ for my own kind purposes. Such is the glory of my grace, my free gift to you in the Beloved, in whom, through his blood, you gain your freedom, the forgiveness of sins. I will bring everything together under Christ, as head, everything in the heavens and everything on earth. And it is in him that you were claimed as my own, chosen from the beginning, stamped with the seal of the Holy Spirit of the Promise, the pledge of your inheritance which brings freedom for you whom I have chosen as my own" (paraphrase of Eph 1:3–14).

Brother Bernard and the Angel

ONCE, when I was returning from a pilgrimage to the shrine of St. James of Compostella, a wondrous thing happened. I was standing on the bank of a wide river that I could not cross when a handsome young man greeted me in Italian, saying "God give you peace, good brother."

I was amazed at the young man's joyful, handsome face, his peaceful manner, and the familiarity of his language, so I asked him, "Where do you come from, my good young man?"

"I come from where Blessed Francis lives," he replied. And then he added, "But why, dear man, do you hesitate to cross this river?"

"Because. I am afraid of the dangerous depth of the water."

And the young man said, "Let us, then, go across together. Do not hesitate."

Then he took my hand and, in the blinking of an eye, placed me on the other side.

I knew then that the young man was an angel of the Lord, so I said with great devotion, reverence, and joy, "Blessed angel of God, tell me, what is your name."

"Brother, do not ask me my name, for it is marvelous."

And with that, he vanished, leaving me deeply comforted, so that I went on my way filled with trust and joy. ❧

ANGELS, MIRACULOUS RIVER CROSSINGS—sometimes it is all so unbelievable. Maybe we just don't recognize these things in our lives. Maybe the Lord does still send us angels in disguise to fan us back to life and joy. And maybe they are not angels at all, but human beings who help us around or through some difficulty we could not have borne without them. Sadly though, it is often only when they leave that we realize the gift they were in our lives, beings through whom God ministered to us.

Lord, thank you for all those in my life who have been like angels to me. And let me be open to those future angels you will surely send to help me on my way, to help me across the waters I still have to ford. And help me to recognize your messengers when you send them, even when they are but flesh and blood like me.

Brother Elias and the Angel

NCE, when Blessed Francis, Brother Masseo, a few of the other brothers, and myself were living in a remote place, a young man came to the door and knocked long and impatiently. Francis was deep in the woods praying and could not hear the knocking, so Brother Masseo answered the door.

"Young man, you must not have been to a friary before; don't you know how to knock gently?"

But the young man replied, "No, how should it be done?"

"Knock three times with a short interval between each knocking. Then wait for as long as it would take someone to say the Our Father, and then if no one comes, knock again in the same way."

"But I am in a hurry, for I have a long way to go. I came to speak with Brother Francis, but he is in the woods praying. Therefore, ask Brother Elias to come, for I have heard he is very wise, and I have a question to put to him."

So Brother Masseo came in to me and told me of the young man and his request. But I became angry and annoyed and would not go.

Poor Brother Masseo was then hard put to find what to do or say, and in the meantime the young man began impatiently beating on the door again. So Brother Masseo went out to him and said, "Why didn't you knock the way I showed you?"

Now, the young man, who was really an angel and knew what had happened in the friary, said, "So—Brother Elias won't come. Go then to Brother Francis and tell him I'm here; but because I don't want to disturb him, tell him he is to send Brother Elias to me."

Then Brother Masseo went and told Francis everything; and without even lowering his eyes from heaven, the saint said, "Tell Brother Elias that under holy obedience he is to go to the door."

Brother Masseo told me what Francis directed, and so I went in a great temper and opened the door violently and noisily.

"What do you want?" I demanded.

"Beware, dear friend," said the young man. "For you are apparently very angry, and anger blinds the soul and keeps it from seeing the truth."

"Just tell me what you want!" I yelled.

"I want to know whether those who follow the Gospel can eat what is set before them, as Christ said, and whether anyone can impose on them something contrary to Gospel freedom?"

"I know the answer to that alright, but why should I tell you? You should mind your own business."

But the young man replied, "Actually I know the answer better than you do."

Then I slammed the door and went away. Soon, however, I began to feel troubled and remembered that as Francis' vicar, I had once imposed upon the brothers something contrary to the Gospel and their Rule—namely, that they eat no meat of any kind. I then remembered the young man's modest manner and how he had said he knew the answer better than I did myself, and I suddenly realized that the question was aimed directly at me.

With that, I returned and opened the door, but there was no one there. Nor could the young man be found anywhere, for he was an angel of God and had departed because he was not welcomed. ❧

THERE IS A ZEN SAYING that goes like this: "Before you can learn to contemplate, you must learn to close doors quietly."

That surely is one of the lessons of this story. For if Brother Elias had learned that lesson, he would have been open to the young man from the beginning, perhaps even teaching him, as Brother Masseo did, how to knock gently.

But Brother Elias had not yet dealt with the violence in himself, and so he answered loud knocking with an equally loud and violent opening of the door. He answered an implied accusation with further anger and a slamming of the door.

Lord, teach me to see without, as well as within. I, too, have at times failed to recognize those "angels," your messengers, who tell me the truth about myself. Help me to temper anger with love.

Brother Bonizzo, Witness to the Rule of Life

HERE is a story that when Francis came to write the final version of his Rule of Life, the Lord himself confirmed it for him. This I know because I, Brother Bonizzo, went with the blessed Father Francis and Brother Leo to the hermitage of Fonte Colombo in the Rieti Valley. There on that mountain, like Moses on Mount Sinai, Blessed Francis received from the Lord a way of life for us, his brothers.

Though the Lord did not give the Rule to Francis as he gave the tablets of the Law to Moses, he confirmed in a vision to Francis that his Rule of Life was indeed from the Lord himself. The Lord assured Francis that the Rule of Life, which we had been living for years and which Francis was now dictating to Brother Leo at Fonte Colombo, was indeed an outline and summary of the call that Francis had received from the Lord, even from the beginning when he spoke to him from the crucifix of San Damiano.

That is why Francis could write with such assurance in his last will and testament, "It was the Lord who gave me brothers, and no one else; and it was the Most High and no one else who showed me what to do, revealing to me that I should live according to the form of the Holy Gospel. This I had written down simply and in few words, and the Lord Pope confirmed it for me." ✦

THE FINAL RULE of St. Francis (dating from 1223) is one of the shortest rules in the history of the Catholic Church. There are only twelve brief chapters, resembling guidelines for those who live a mendicant, itinerant life—it is a sort of compendium of "tips for the road," as in St. Francis' words in Chapter 3: "I advise, admonish, and exhort you in the Lord Jesus Christ that when you travel through the world you do not quarrel or argue or judge others; rather, be meek, peaceful and modest, courteous and humble, speaking honorably to everyone."

THE VERSE KING

HERE was a man from the Marches of Ancona who was known as the King of Verses. He was a vain troubadour, one who composed and sang ballads and verses of love, some noble and some impure. And so good was he at his art that he had once been crowned the Verse King by the Emperor himself.

I was that man. And once, when I was visiting a relative of mine, a Benedictine nun in the town of San Severino, in God's Providence, Blessed Francis was also there, preaching in the convent chapel. Out of curiosity and to satisfy my kinswoman, I stood in the rear of the chapel and tried to listen as the Blessed Francis preached. But the words Francis spoke were so foreign to me that I was about to leave when I beheld a marvelous vision: there appeared upon Francis' body two glittering swords in the form of a cross, one vertical from head to foot, and the other horizontal from one hand to the other across his breast.

And then I recognized who this Francis was, the one they called "God's Troubadour," because he sang God's praises in French and was known to sing and dance through city and forest like the troubadour's own jongleur.

And so I began to listen with what seemed another, inner ear to what Francis was saying. And as I listened I resolved to improve my life, not right then, but sometime in the future. But that was not to be, for when Blessed Francis finished preaching, he turned the sword of God's word upon me personally. He took me aside and first gently admonished me about the vanity of the world and then moved me deeply by showing me where my life of sin was leading.

I said right there and then, "What need have I of more words? Let us have deeds. Take me from among people and give me back to the Great Emperor."

The next day, Francis invested me and gave me the name Brother Pacifico, because I had been brought back to the peace of God. And my conversion and investiture as a friar had a profound effect upon people because I was so famous in all the region of the Marches.

And to the end, I continued to be visited by special

favors and visions, including a vision of Francis in which the saint bore upon his forehead the sign of the elect in the prophecy of Ezekiel, the Greek letter *tau*, which radiated from many-colored circles the beauty of the peacock.

The Lord also gifted me with the interpretation of visions, such as the one Francis himself related to me. It happened, he said, one night after he had been in prayer for a long time and sleep had finally overtaken him. In the vision, his soul was escorted into the sanctuary of God, and he saw there, as in a dream, a beautiful, elegant woman. Her head seemed to be of gold, her bosom and arms of silver, her abdomen of crystal, and the rest of her body from the waist down, of iron. She was tall and delicate and symmetrically fashioned, but over her beautiful body she wore a soiled mantle.

When Francis told his dream to me, he did not explain what it meant. And though I gave my own interpretation at the time, who is to say it is the only one? Some, for example, have already begun to interpret the beautiful woman as Lady Poverty, the spouse of Blessed Francis, whereas I interpreted the dream this way: the beautiful woman is the soul of our Father Francis; the head is golden to represent his contemplation and wisdom; the silver bosom and arms are the words of the Lord, which Blessed Francis meditated on in his heart and fulfilled in his actions; the crystal, because it is hard, signifies sobriety, and because it is bright, chastity; the iron is his perseverance; and the soiled mantle is his despised little body, which covers his precious soul.

I have interpreted this vision thus because Blessed Francis refused to interpret it, which he would not have done if the vision had referred to something or someone other than himself. ✦

Lᴏʀᴅ, I ꜱᴇᴇ ɴᴏ ᴠɪꜱɪᴏɴꜱ, but I do dream, both sleeping and waking, and I do try to love you with all my heart, even if I can't always see how beautiful my own soul is.

Sometimes my soul's face seems ugly and repulsive. It is hard for me to embrace that ugliness and kiss it. Transform me into precious stones and metals.

Tʜᴇ Bʀᴏᴛʜᴇʀ Wʜᴏ Wᴀɴᴛᴇᴅ ᴛᴏ Bᴇ ᴀ Sᴏʟɪᴛᴀʀʏ Pɪʟɢʀɪᴍ

HERE was a certain brother renowned for his holiness both within the Order and among the people of his region, who decided he needed greater solitude for prayer and devotion. The brother separated himself from his brothers in the Order. He took off his cowl and shortened his habit and began to roam the earth as a solitary pilgrim in search of a deeper union with God.

But much to his dismay, in his new, solitary life, the Lord withdrew his consolation, and a storm of temptations entered the brother's heart. He had nowhere to turn for encouragement and support and he was near despair. But then insight and understanding rose up within him, and he came to his senses.

"Return to your brothers," he said to himself, "for *there* is your salvation."

Then without delay, he hurried back to find his brother, like a child in search of his mother's breast.

Now, the first place of the brothers that he came upon was in Siena, and Francis happened to be staying there. But when the holy friar saw the former brother approaching, he immediately fled from him and shut himself up in this cell. This surprised the brothers greatly, because Francis was always merciful and kind toward those who sought forgiveness. They therefore asked their father, Francis, why he had fled from the repentant brother.

"Why do you ask such a question? Did you not know that I fled to the protection of prayer to deliver our erring brother? I saw in my son what displeased me, so I went immediately to Christ, who alone can forgive and who alone can deliver us from our delusions."

Then the brother came and knelt in shame at Francis' feet and confessed his guilt.

And Francis said, "May the Lord forgive you, brother. And from now on, beware lest you be tricked again to separate yourself from your brothers and to believe that greater holiness is elsewhere."

And from that day on, I, who am that same brother, dwelt ever among my brothers, and that has been more than enough for me. ❧

Lord, sometimes the temptation to strike out on my own is very strong. I can't see how my present life with my family, or my brothers and sisters in community, is allowing me to grow. Everyone around me seems only a distraction or a burden, and I wish I could just leave everything and everyone and be free.

But that is only a temptation most of the time, Lord. For I find you in my commitments and responsibilities, my loves and friendships, not in fleeing them. And in finding you, I find myself. You are where I am, not somewhere else. Lord Jesus, help me to discover you here where I am.

Another Tale of
Brother Pacifico

NCE, when Francis and some of us were passing through the countryside between Cannara and Bevagna near Assisi, we saw a marvelous sight. There in the trees beside the road was a multitude of birds of various kinds and colors, some of which had never been seen before in that region. And in the fields there were even more birds, so that the whole countryside seemed alive with wings and birdsong.

Now, Francis, who seemed to know the secret language of all living things, looked upon this incredible scene, turned to us brothers, and said, "Dear brothers, I ask you to wait here while I go and preach to our sisters the birds." Then he went into the field and began to preach.

Immediately all the birds stopped singing and those in the trees flew down into the field at Francis' feet. And though he walked among them, brushing them with his robe, the birds remained silent and did not move as he said, "O my Sister Birds, how grateful you should be for all the Lord has given you, for the gift of flying free and for your double and triple plumage, colored and designed by him. Praise him, too, for the nourishment he sets out for you without your having to procure it. Praise him for the song he's given you, and for the way your Creator increases your number. Praise him for preserving you in the ark and for the element of air he has set apart for you. You neither sow nor reap, yet God feeds you; gives you streams and rivers to drink from; mountains, hills, rocks, and caves to hide in; trees in which to build your nests. And though you cannot spin or weave, he clothes you.

"So much blessing shows, my sisters, how much he loves you. Take care then, dear sisters, not to be ungrateful, but to praise and thank your Creator always."

Then all the birds began to sing and beat their wings and stretch their necks and bow low before Blessed Francis, so pleased were they with his words. And Francis began praising God, joining the birds in praising their Creator. And he asked me, Brother Pacifico, to sing along, and the other brothers too. Then, as he made the sign of the cross over his sisters, they all soared into the air and dispersed in the four directions of the cross, east, west, north, and south, committing themselves to the Providence of God. ✦

LORD, I WISH I KNEW the language of birds, of plants and animals, that I, too, might invite them to sing your praises! But I don't. Yet, I can praise you for them and through them. I can sing of creatures and praise you in the words you yourself gave us.

> Let the earth bless the Lord:
> praise and glorify him for ever!
>
> Bless the Lord, mountains and hills,
> praise and glorify him for ever!
>
> Bless the Lord, every plant that grows,
> praise and glorify him for ever!
>
> Bless the Lord, springs of water,
> praise and glorify him for ever!
>
> Bless the Lord, seas and rivers,
> praise and glorify him for ever!
>
> Bless the Lord, whales and everything
>   that moves in the waters,
> praise and glorify him for ever!
>
> Bless the Lord, every kind of bird,
> praise and glorify him for ever!
>
> Bless the Lord, all animals wild and tame,
> praise and glorify him for ever!

(Dn 3:74–81)

OF GRECCIO AND THE FIRST CHRISTMAS CRIB

OW cold it seemed that December. Not that winters aren't always cold here, with Mount Terminillo towering above our small village of Greccio. But that December seemed particularly cold, and not only outside, but inside, too, in the heart. It was as if a fire had burned out, some vision had blurred into a fine, freezing mist upon the mountain.

That was December of 1223, the year Francis, the saint from Assisi, was spending Christmas with his brothers in the hermitage on the mountain opposite our village. And that is what changed the weather, outside and in.

One day, as Christmas drew near, Francis sent for me, a citizen of Greccio, and asked me to prepare a manger scene in the little hermitage where the brothers were to celebrate Midnight Mass of the Nativity. He asked that I bring a real ox and ass to stand beside the rock that was to serve as the altar. And so I did.

And then, on Christmas Eve, we townspeople, invited by Francis and his brothers, made our way to the hermitage. We carried torches down the steep side of the hill where our proud village stands, down into the valley, and up the other side to where the brothers waited in prayer in the small cave that looked for all the world the way I had imagined the cave of Bethlehem.

Francis was clothed in the dalmatic, his deacon's vestment, and we knew then that he would be singing the Gospel, as is the deacon's function at a Solemn Mass. And so sweet was Francis' voice as he sang the Gospel that we all wept. Then Francis preached as well, and so sweet and warm were his words that it was no longer cold in the cave or in our hearts. Indeed, this must have been what the shepherds felt at Bethlehem so long ago.

As the Mass continued our song grew to such a crescendo of jubilee that there appeared upon the altars of our souls a multitude of the heavenly host, singing "Glory to God in the highest, and peace to all of goodwill." And we knelt in adoration waiting for that precious moment when the Infant Christ would become the bread and wine upon the altar.

And so it came to pass—and more! For at the moment of consecration the Christ Child appeared alive upon the rock altar. And Blessed Francis leaned down and lifted the child in his arms like Simeon of old. And that is the miracle of Greccio you may have heard about.

Not everyone saw it, as I did, but everyone there felt their hearts burn within them and warm weather return to the winter of their disbelief. Bethlehem was now Greccio in the Rieti Valley.

I praise and bless God for the small part I played in this new Bethlehem, I, John Vellita, the man who brought the ox and the ass and made a place where the Baby Jesus could speak to our hearts again, Baby Jesus, the little Word that grows into the big Word of Jesus the Christ, who is God come among us. Amen. ✠

THE MIRACLE OF GRECCIO began the tradition of the Christmas Crib. Lord, on Christmas Day I feel my heart burning with hope and love and renewed faith. I feel with St. Francis this Christmas psalm he composed which I now make my own:

Sing for joy to God our strength,
acclaim the Lord God living and true with shouts of joy.
For Yahweh, the Most High, is glorious,
the great king over all the earth.

Because the Most Holy Father of Heaven, our king from
the first, sent his beloved Son from on high and he was
born of the blessed, holy Virgin Mary.
"He will cry to me, 'You are my father.' So I shall
make him my first-born, the highest of earthly kings."
On that day the Lord bestowed his mercy and that night
his song.

This is the day which Yahweh has made,
a day for us to rejoice and be glad.
For the Most Holy Beloved Child was given to us and was
born for us on the way and laid in a manger, because
there was no room at the inn.

✓ Of Perfect Joy

OW many times we walked to Perugia and back to Our Lady of the Angels, often in the rain or snow. Sometimes there would be a few disgruntled souls along the way who would glare hatefully and scoff at us for not working in the fields or shops like honest folk. And I was always angered by their taunts and would want to explain that we were on a mission of preaching, but Francis would always stop me and say, "Brother Leo, if we have to explain what we are doing, then we are not preaching at all."

"But," I would argue, "can't you see, holy father, that these people don't understand? They think we are lazy wastrels living off their kindness."

"Brother Leo! But that is even better, for that is perfect joy."

And then would begin his poem of perfect joy, which I had heard many times before but never seemed to grasp fully, just as the people along our way never seemed to really grasp what we were about.

"Brother Leo, do you know what perfect joy is?"

"Yes, holy father, but tell me again, for apparently I have forgotten once more."

"Indeed you have, dear brother, or you'd not have been tempted to defend our life to those who scoff at us and hurl all manner of abuse at us."

"Tell me, then, holy father, where is the joy in all this

misunderstanding and abuse and walking barefoot in the melting snow and mud?"

"Leo, even if the people were edified by us and remarked how holy we were, nevertheless—write down and mark well—that is not perfect joy."

The first few times we had this little walking dialogue, I asked immediately, "What is perfect joy, then, Father Francis?" But after a while I only walked in silence at the side of Francis', who, no matter what I might have said, would have pursued his story to the end, saying at regular intervals "No, Brother Leo, even if we gave sight to the blind, cured the lame, drove out devils, restored hearing to the deaf, made cripples walk and the mute talk, and even woke the dead—write down and mark well—that is not perfect joy."

And we would walk on in silence until Blessed Francis, as if he had been continuing the story in his own mind, would break in again, "No, Brother Leo, even if we brothers spoke all languages and possessed all wisdom and knew the whole Bible and could reveal the future and knew the secrets of hearts—mark well—that is not perfect joy."

And again we would walk on in silence until Blessed Francis thought I could not take the suspense any longer, and he would cry aloud, "No, Brother Leo, God's little lamb, even if we spoke with the tongues of angels and knew the courses of the stars and the powers of herbs, and all the treasures of the earth were revealed to us, including the properties and powers of birds and beasts and fishes, of humans and trees and stones and roots and water—write down and continue to mark well—that is not perfect joy."

I then would usually allow him about an hour of additional embellishments that were not perfect joy, such as "No, Brother Leo, even if we Lesser Brothers could preach so that all the faithless would be converted to the faith of Christ—mark well—neither is that perfect joy."

And then, weary with walking and listening, I would pretend exasperation and say, "Father, I beg you, for God's sake, tell me, what is perfect joy?"

And his answer always had to do with suffering something for the love of Jesus Christ. But the one that moved me the most—and was, according to Francis himself, the best answer he ever gave—came on a cold winter day when we were returning from Perugia and were just about to reach our beloved Portiuncula.

"Well, Brother Leo, listen well. When we come to the Portiuncula and are wet to the bone with mud and weak with hunger, and we knock on the friary door, and the Brother Porter answers and is angry and says, 'Who are you?' and we say, 'We are two of your brothers,' and he says, 'You're lying. You're really two robbers who go about deceiving people and stealing the alms of the poor. Out with you!' . . . and when he speaks that way to us and refuses to open the door but lets us stand there hungry in the cold and snow and water, with night falling, and we endure his abusive words and his wicked treatment, endure it without becoming angry and without quarreling with him, but instead think in humility and love that Brother Porter knows us as we really are and that God is the one who lets him talk to us like that, Brother Leo—that is perfect joy.

"And if we keep on knocking so that Brother Porter comes out and angrily drives us away like a couple of thieves, boxing our ears and cursing us and saying 'Get out of here, you worthless leeches, go to the lepers, because you're not going to get any food or lodging here.' And we bear this, too, patiently and cheerfully and with charity, Brother Leo, mark well—that is perfect joy.

"And if, driven by the cold and hunger and the threat of night, we knock again and beg with bitter tears that for God's sake he let us in, if only just inside the door, and he grows even more angry and says, 'What kind of shameless people are you, anyway? Maybe this will convince you!' And he runs out with a knobby club and seizes us by the cowls and throws us to the ground and rolls us in the snow and comes close to clubbing us to death; and if we endure all this patiently, thinking only of the sufferings of Christ, to whom belongs all praise, and how much we should suffer for the sake of our love for him, Brother Leo—that is perfect joy.

"Now, listen well to the ending, Brother Leo! Greater than any grace or gift of the Holy Spirit is Christ's gift to his friends of conquering self and willingly enduring suffering, injustice, contempt, and harshness. For we cannot take any credit for the other gifts of God, because they are not ours; they come from God. But we can take credit for trials, sufferings, and crosses. With the Apostle Paul we can all say that there is nothing we can glory in, except in carrying the cross of our Lord Jesus Christ."

Now, of all the words that Francis spoke, this story of perfect joy contains the secret of who he was and why he lived the way he did. It explains to those who can hear why cold and snow and mud and biting rain and dark night were bright and warm and softly beautiful to the Blessed Francis. ✦

W HAT AN EXTRAORDINARY story this is! And how contradictory to almost everything most of us think will make us happy. It almost seems masochistic of St. Francis to say such negative things about joy. And yet, the whole passage echoes St. Paul's paean to charity in First Corinthians, verse 13, except that Francis' version dramatizes the suffering that cannot overcome love.

As with St. Paul, the whole reason behind Francis' insistence on enduring the blows of life patiently, is charity, the love of Christ, who suffered like things for love of us. That is the secret of perfect joy: celebrating everything, even suffering, for love of Christ, who first loved us. Always Francis keeps Christ Crucified before his eyes. That is his secret and ours, too, if we are to know perfect joy.

WINGS

N the summer of 1224, Francis' eye sickness began to improve, enabling him to leave Rieti and go to the mountain retreat of La Verna in Tuscany, north of Assisi. This was the mountain that Count Orlando of Chiusi gave to Blessed Francis and us brothers for our use, that we might have a place of total quiet and seclusion where we could pray undisturbed.

Two years before his death, aware that the end of his earthly days was near, Francis wanted to celebrate at La Verna the Feast of the Assumption of Our Lady, which falls on August 15. Afterward he would begin a fast of forty days in preparation for the Feast of St. Michael the Archangel on September 29.

Taking with him his companions Leo, Masseo, Sylvester, Illuminato, and me, Angelo, Francis set out on foot from Assisi, for La Verna. But shortly after we began, Francis' health started to fail again, and he became so weak that we had to seek out a peasant's hut in order to beg the use of a donkey for Francis to ride upon. So when we saw smoke rising in the evening sky, we went up to the hut and knocked on the door. A peasant answered, and when he heard our request, he looked at Francis and asked if he was the Francis of Assisi he'd heard so much about? And when we assured him he was holy Father Francis, the man said, "Well, then, Francis of Assisi, be sure you are as good as they say you are, for there are many who have faith in you!" Then Francis fell at the peasant's feet and kissed them and thanked the man for his reminder.

We then went on our way and came at last to the holy mountain, La Verna, where Francis separated himself from us by crossing over a little ravine by use of a wooden plank that could be removed like a drawbridge. He instructed Brother Leo to come twice daily, once during the day to bring a bit of bread and water, and once during the night at the hour of matins. When Brother Leo approached, he was to say, "O Lord, open my lips," and if Francis answered, "And my mouth shall declare your praise," Brother Leo was to approach. But if there was no response, Brother Leo was to depart and leave Francis to the silence of his prayer.

It was at this spot, on the Feast of the Exaltation of the Holy Cross, September 14, that an extraordinary event took place. Francis, led by the Holy Spirit, prayed these words he had composed in preparation for the feast: "O Lord, I beg of you two graces before I die: to experience personally and in all possible fullness the pains of your bitter passion, and to feel for you the same love that moved you to sacrifice yourself for us."

And as he prayed, Francis was facing east with his arms stretched out, and there, coming down from heaven, appeared a six-winged seraph. As it neared, Francis saw that it resembled a man with two wings in flight, two wings covering his body, and two wings raised above his head. And with a rush of love and pity, Francis saw that the seraph's features were those of the crucified Lord Jesus Christ, who had spoken to him from the crucifix of San Damiano so many years before and whose image he had kept embla-zoned on his heart all these years.

Love overcame him. And when he awoke, he felt blood running from an open wound in his left side and his hands were pierced with nails, their black heads protruding from his palms and their points bent over as with a hammer on the backs of his hands, so that they looked like little rings close pressed to the skin. And his feet, too, were pierced with nails, only now the heads of the nails were on his insteps and the points bent over on his soles, so that he wondered how he was going to walk. And indeed from that moment until his death two years later, Francis walked only with the greatest pain, and most of the time he had to be carried or travel by donkey.

Thus was it that Francis' prayer to the Crucified One was answered. He was forever sealed with the Father's love, transforming him into a living image of the Father's only Son, Jesus Christ. And Francis became in his suffering what he already was in so many other ways, a mirror of our Savior, Jesus Christ.

To all of this I attest, Brother Angelo Tancredi, former knight, now a Knight of Christ, through his mercy and the inspiration of his servant Francis. ❧

LORD, I DON'T KNOW IF I have the courage to pray as St. Francis did, to experience the fullness of your suffering in my own body and soul, nor do I think I could bear to feel the same love for you as that which moved you to suffer and die for me. How much I would need to expand and deepen before I could make so awesome a prayer. I can, however, pray for some measure of what St. Francis prayed for, to experience something of your bitter passion, whatever you think I can bear, and to feel a portion of the love that moved you to suffer and die for me.

I cannot begin to grasp in my mind or in my heart what so much love means, let alone carry it in my body. I do not want the pain nor do I feel I understand it really. It seems beyond my comprehension. Love and pain—Lord, teach me gently of these.

A Letter to Brother Leo

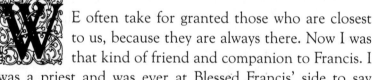E often take for granted those who are closest to us, because they are always there. Now I was that kind of friend and companion to Francis. I was a priest and was ever at Blessed Francis' side to say Mass and hear his confession and be privy to his most intimate thoughts and concerns. There are many stories about Francis and me, and I have even written down my memoirs of the holy father. But there is one story in particular that speaks to the very heart of who we were to one another. ·

We were at La Verna, that strange and mystical mountain where, two years before he died, Blessed Francis received the wounds of Christ. It was shortly after Francis had received the Holy Stigmata, and we were deeply absorbed in silent meditation, the prayer of the mountain.

Having been friends for many years, we knew éach other well, and I had learned to give Francis the distance he needed to enter more deeply into prayer. I guarded over his solitude always, but on this particular occasion, as Francis continued to pray for days on end, lost in God, I was having a difficult time with in an intense spiritual battle within myself that seemed to get worse each day. I didn't want to disturb him, but I knew that if I had but the merest word from Francis, I would be strengthened and would be able to bear my anguish of spirit. But, not wanting to betray my promise to Francis to preserve his solitude, I suffered alone and in silence.

Francis, however, saw in his mind's eye what was happening to me, and he called out to me from the deep woods where he was praying.

"Brother Leo, Little Sheep, come here, my dear friend!"

And I, thinking something had befallen the holy father, bounded quickly into the woods where Francis knelt in prayer.

"What is it, dear Father? Are you all right?"

"Of course I am, Little Sheep. How could I not be with you here?"

Francis always called me Brother Pecorella, which means Little Sheep, or when he was more playful, Brother Pecorone, which means Big Sheep, but also has the figurative meaning of Blockhead. Now, that Francis would use such an appellation for his dearest friend shows how close we really were, for I had a very large head and was naturally quite sensitive about it; and yet, I was always deeply touched whenever Francis called me this—especially this time, when I was in such a depression and feeling so low.

"Oh, Brother Pecorone, why did you not come to me and tell me that you wanted some words of encouragement from me?"

I was stunned, though I shouldn't have been, that Francis should know my deepest thoughts, and said, "Dear holy Father, I was afraid to disturb the Lord's working in you or trespass upon his most holy presence."

"But, Little Sheep, did you not know that you are his presence for me and all the brothers? And did you not know that the Lord would want me to interrupt our holy dialogue to minister to one who all these years has never asked for anything for himself but to serve God and our brotherhood?"

"You humble me, dear Father, for only now I was feeling ugly and sad and taken for granted. I was feeling sorry for myself that I had to suffer alone while you, dear Father, were rapt in spiritual ecstasy. Please forgive me."

"Ah, how little you still know of me. I was in fact also suffering inner torment and feeling sorry for myself because of what I see as the brothers' betrayal of Lady Poverty in their building of friaries that are not in keeping with their poor spouse. And the Lord himself showed me *your* suffering and how much he loves you, not just because of all you have borne for him, but because you are you, the work of his hands. And so moved was I by the Lord's goodness in creating such as you, Brother Leo, that I wrote a Magnificat of praise for so good a God."

Then, to my great delight, Francis took the paper with his praises of God on it and, turning it over, penned these words: "May the Lord bless you and keep you! May the Lord show his face to you and be merciful to you! May the Lord lift up his countenance upon you and give you peace! God bless you, Brother Leo!"

Francis was then just about to give the paper to me when he paused and put it down again and sketched a crude head, a sort of Pecorone, and drew the letter *tau* (τ) issuing from the mouth of the head. And he said, handing me the paper, "Take this, dear Little Sheep, and keep it with you as long as you live."

Then, seeing myself signed with the *tau*, the sign of the elect, and receiving this precious gift from Francis, I was immediately freed of my depression and it never troubled me again. I kissed the holy parchment and placed it in the pocket next to 'my heart and I carried it with me for the remaining forty years of my life. And every day I would take it out and read Francis' blessing and look at the Pecorone, beautiful because Francis drew it for me, so that I would remember how much God loves even the Pecoroni of this world. And then I would turn the parchment over and pray the praises of God, which Francis wrote in ecstasy. And this is what I prayed:

> You are holy, Lord,
> God alone, who works marvels.
> You are strong and grand and most High.

You are the All-Powerful, Holy Father,
King of heaven and earth.

You are three and one, Lord God of gods.

You are the Good, every good, the highest good,
the Lord God, living and true.

You are love, charity, wisdom, humility, patience.

You are beauty, safety, and rest.

You are joy and gladness.

You are our hope and our justice and our temperance.

You are all our treasure overflowing.

You are beauty and meekness.

You are our protector, our guardian and defender.

You are strength and refreshment.

You are our hope, our faith, our charity.

You are all our sweetness.

You are our eternal great and wondrous Lord,
God All-Powerful, merciful Savior.

Sᴛ. Fʀᴀɴᴄɪs' ᴡʜᴏʟᴇ ʟɪFᴇ was a reaching for the heights where the Most High dwells. But the way he took was through creatures, reaching out to them, and joining with them in praise and love of God. Francis reaches out to Brother Leo in his confusion and pain and anoints him with the *tau*, the sign of the elect, and teaches Leo how to pray by putting aside self-pity and self-absorption and fixing one's eyes on God.

Lord, teach me to pray. Help me to learn to focus my eyes and heart on you where you dwell in all of creation: in things, in plants and animals, in people.

St. Francis Sings His Swan Song

HEN Father Francis came down from Mount La Verna, the wounds of Christ he had received from the seraph caused him exceeding joy but also great pain. And because his eye sickness had worsened, he was nearly blind and could not bear the sun by day nor a candle by night, so great was the pain that all light caused him. He was discouraged as well by his brothers' increasing betrayals of Lady Poverty as they began to build friaries and to depart bit by bit from the poor and simple Gospel life that the Lord himself had shown him.

Thus, broken as he was in body and spirit, Francis did not go immediately to where the brothers awaited him at the Portiuncula, but he came instead to me, his sister Clare, and to the Poor Ladies at San Damiano. There I had a small hut built for him next to our chapel, and he entered this cave of reeds and rushes and remained there in darkness for over fifty days, unable to rest even at night because of the pain in his eyes and the field mice that ran back and forth across his broken body.

Night and day he suffered, unable to rest, until one day I heard him pray, "Lord Jesus Christ, Good Shepherd, grant me, your little sheep, grace and virtue so that I will not depart from you, no matter what my trouble, tribulation, or grief may be."

Then he heard a voice from heaven speaking to him:

"Francis, answer me. If the whole world should turn to gold, and the sea, rivers, and springs become balm, and all the mountains, stones, and springs should turn into gems, but you found a treasure greater than them to the degree that gold is more precious than all of them and balm more precious than water, gems than mountains and rocks, and if all that precious treasure were given you in exchange for your present suffering, would you not rejoice?"

And our father replied, "Lord, I am not worthy of such a treasure."

But the Lord said, "But I have already set aside such a treasure for you, eternal life. And if I clothe you now with sickness and infirmity, you should rejoice in it, for it is my pledge of that blessed treasure."

Then Father Francis, his soul warmed and his body taking strength, broke into this canticle:

Highest, all powerful, good Lord,
Yours is the praise, the glory, and the honor,
And every blessing.
They belong to You alone,
And no one is worthy to speak Your Name.

So, praised be You, My Lord, with all Your creatures,
Especially Sir Brother Sun,
Who makes the day and enlightens us through You.
He is lovely and radiant and grand;
And he heralds You, his Most High Lord.

Praised be You, my Lord, through Sister Moon
and stars.
You have hung them in heaven shining and precious and
fair.
And praise to You, my Lord, through Brother Wind,

In air and cloud, calm, and every weather
That sustains Your creatures.

Praised be You, my Lord, through Sister Water,
So very useful, humble, precious, and chaste.

Yes, and praise to You, my Lord, through Brother Fire.
Through him You illumine our night,
And he is handsome and merry, robust and strong.

Praised be You, my Lord, through our Sister, Mother
Earth,
Who nourishes us and teaches us,
Bringing forth all kinds of fruits and colored flowers
and herbs.

We stood about in wonder at the beauty of Francis' song, as well as at the sound of his voice singing again after so many days in despair. He was once again the troubadour, and this, we knew, was his swan song, the words that summed up a troubadour's life. ❧

LIKE EVERY TROUBADOUR at the end of his life, St. Francis, too, sang the song that was all his songs in one. More even than his last testament, these words of his "Canticle of Brother Sun" say who he had become, one for whom everything was brother or sister. He became a tongue to praise God for all those creatures who cannot articulate, as humans can, their gratitude. He returned to God what God had first given him, the whole of creation to cherish.

Lord, what is my song? Teach me the words that sum up

who I am. And when my work on earth is done, let me praise you with my own voice and sing back to you the song you planted in my soul when you created me.

A Song for the Poor Ladies

FROM the moment our father began to sing again, he changed, even in his relationship with us, the Poor Ladies of San Damiano. Before, his visits to us were rare, and when he did come, he said little and left quickly. On one occasion, for example, he came to preach the word of God to us, but when we were all gathered to hear him, he did not address us; he raised his eyes to heaven and asked for some ashes, which he sprinkled on the floor in a circle around him. Then he poured some on his head and stood there in silence for what seemed like hours, though it was but a few moments. When he opened his lips to speak, it was as if he spoke to a face beyond us, saying "Have mercy on me, O God, in your faithful love." These opening lines of Psalm 51, he continued to sing to the end. Then he left, having said nothing directly to us at all, though by his presence we came to understand the words of the psalmist he had enacted before us.

But how different it was once the whole tapestry of his life was woven and displayed in his "Canticle." From then on, he seemed freed of everything that had kept him bound up before. He knew with certainty that everything was gift, including eternity. And he entered a whole new dimension, living in heaven almost, so that he appeared less worried about how he would be interpreted by others. He was done with placing heavy burdens upon himself. Nor did he need to be as reserved as he had been with us. In fact, he wrote a song for us, and these are its words:

> Listen, little poor ones, called by the Lord and
> drawn together from many regions and provinces;
> live always by the truth,
> that you may die in obedience.
> Do not look outward for life;
> the life of the Spirit within is better.
> With great love I beg you
> to use discreetly
> the alms the Lord gives you.
> Those of you oppressed with sickness
> and you others wearied with caring for them,
> all of you: bear it in peace.
> For this fatigue you will sell at a very high price,
> and in heaven each of you will be crowned a queen
> with the Virgin Mary.

How much joy this song gave us! In his words and music, as in his previous silence, he gave us himself. And both were good because both were the stuff of who he was. ❧

THE WORDS ST. FRANCIS WROTE for St. Clare and the Poor Ladies were lost for centuries, much to the sorrow of the followers of St. Clare. Then, in 1976, Franciscan Father Giovanni Boccali found the lost song in two manuscripts in Verona, Italy.

Lord, do not let our song be lost. It is our destiny to sing, for if we cannot be a song of peace and happiness of soul to those around us, we have failed. And let not our ashes lie mute, but let our very molecules become eternal songs of praise to you, manuscripts of peopled-notes, never lost, never silenced.

THE PHYSICIAN'S TALE

HERE are many stories about Francis that took place here in the Rieti Valley, at the foot of the Sabine hills between Rome and Assisi. My town of Rieti is surrounded by Poggio Bustone, Greccio, and Fonte Colombo, the mountain hermitages of Blessed Francis. At Poggio Bustone, Francis was assured by an angel of the Lord that all his sins were forgiven. At Greccio, Francis started the custom of the Christmas crib by recreating the Bethlehem scene at Midnight Mass. And at Fonte Colombo, Francis wrote his Rule of Life.

It was also at Fonte Colombo that Francis' eyes were cauterized by me, a physician from Rieti. While Francis was in the East preaching and trying to bring peace to Crusaders and Muslims alike, he contracted an eye sickness that was quite painful and left him virtually blind. And he went about with his eyes bandaged because he could not endure light.

Both Brother Elias, Francis' vicar, and his friend, the Papal Protector of the Order, Cardinal Hugolino, persuaded Francis to undergo the painful eye cauterization.

And so Francis went to La Foresta, a fourth hermitage in the Rieti Valley, to retire in prayer in preparation for the operation. Afterward, bandaged about the eyes and mounted on a donkey, Francis was led blind and in darkness to Fonte Colombo, where I awaited him.

Now, when the brothers who were with Francis entered the room and saw the smoking-hot iron, they were overcome and fled from the room in fear. But Francis, in order to strengthen his spirit and overcome fear, said to the fire in which the poker lay, "My Brother Fire, so noble and useful among all creatures, be kind to me in this hour, be courteous, for I have loved you in the past in the Lord. I pray you, dear brother, in the name of him who created you, to temper your heat so that I can bear it."

Then Francis made the sign of the cross over his Brother Fire, and when I laid the red-hot iron to his tender temples from the ear to the eyebrow, to my astonishment he felt no pain at all.

147

The operation over, the brothers came into the room again, and Francis said to them, "O, my fainthearted brothers and men of little faith! Why did you run away in fear? For I felt no pain at all, nor even the heat of the fire. In fact, if this cauterization does not satisfy the doctor, let him do it again."

And, indeed, there was a later cauterization, and again Brother Fire was gentle with the saint, so that he felt no pain. ❧

THERE ARE NUMEROUS REFERENCES in the early sources of St. Francis' reverence for fire, the great symbol of love. Fire is both saving and destroying. It can illumine, but it can also destroy, depending on how it is used or whether or not it is controlled. Fire that does not burn, that illumines but does not consume, is a symbol of the fire of passion that has been purified by love, of the integration of Eros and Agape. That St. Francis does not feel the hot poker used for cauterization symbolizes how deeply he has been purified by love. His desires and passions no longer consume him, because they have been transformed.

Help us, Lord, to enkindle the fire of your love in our hearts so that we will reverence fire and all creatures as our brothers and sisters. For in today's world we have it in us to destroy all creation—earth, water, and air subsumed in a destructive fire of our own making, a fire that splits the very center God put inside all things to hold them together until he comes.

St. Francis and
the Celestial Zither ✓

A T the time Francis was undergoing the treatment for his eyes in the city of Rieti, he spent a few days in the house of Teobaldo Saraceni. He was in great pain, and so he decided to make an unusual request of me, one of his brothers who had played the zither before entering the Order.

"Brother," Francis said, "the children of this world have no understanding of the things of God. There was a time when the zither accompanied the praise of God and consoled the spirit; now it promotes vanity and what is contrary to the Lord's will. But I wish to praise God again in song accompanied by a zither, therefore I want you to secretly borrow one from some good person and play me beautiful music that I can put words to. I have composed some praises of the Lord, and I thought if we sang them aloud, it might change my physical pain into joy and spiritual consolation."

But I answered, "Father, I am ashamed to go looking for a zither, because the people here know what kind of songs I sang when I played this instrument. They might think I have gone back to my old ways."

"In that case, my brother, we need not talk about it any further."

The next night, however, as Francis lay awake at midnight, unable to sleep, he heard a zither beneath his window. It was the sweetest, most exquisite sound he had ever heard. And though the musician withdrew, so Francis could not see his playing, our father could still hear him. Then the musician drew near again and played for a good hour.

Francis, recognizing God's hand at work, was filled with utmost joy and fervently praised the Lord, who had granted him so rare and precious a consolation.

In the morning Francis called us brothers together and said to me in front of everybody, "Brother, I asked you for something you could not grant, but the Lord, who consoles his friends in their tribulations, did for me what you could not do." Then he told us all what had happened, and we were filled with admiration.

We were all convinced that God himself had intervened to console Blessed Francis, because the mayor had decreed that no one was to wander about the city in the middle of the night, even as early as the third ringing of the bells. And Francis himself strengthened our belief by adding that the zither came and went in silence, without words or any vocal sound, and still it consoled his soul for at least an hour. ⋇

Aₛₖ ᴀɴᴅ ʏᴏᴜ ꜱʜᴀʟʟ ʀᴇᴄᴇɪᴠᴇ. Such a simple request, some music, a zither to help him find peace and praise God. Francis asked, but he did not receive at first, because his brother could not overcome shame. God, however, lives by his promises and granted Francis his request, for God knew of it even before the asking.

Lord, such faith! Such love! God and Francis harmonious, together making song.

✓ St. Francis the Solar Hero

NE time when Francis was away and we brothers were praying in the crypt of the Cathedral of San Rufino, we saw a vision. At the very heart of night, when we were deep in prayer, a chariot of light suddenly entered through the little door and circled several times in the air about the room. In the chariot was the sun, and it lit up the room, so that we dazed watchers were amazed. And not only did we see the light borne by the chariot, but we felt our hearts illumined as well. And when the chariot passed out of the room, the light remained and our consciences were revealed to one another.

Then it was that we realized we had seen the soul of our holy Father Francis. He had become the sun-bearer, the illuminator of our souls. And we gave thanks exceedingly for this great grace of God. ✦

THE FRANCISCAN ELOI LECLERC interprets the Francis of this vision as the solar hero of mythology, the symbol of the integrated person. Through this image of the fiery chariot, the storyteller presents us with a Francis whose wild, animal nature, represented by the horses, has been tamed by the divine element, the soul. And now he drives the chariot of the self through the air because he has integrated his lower nature with his spirit. His animal nature now gives his soul the energy to fly, and his soul gives his animal nature the weightlessness of wings.* It is so significant that the great painter Giotto chose this vision as one of the scenes in his series of frescoes in the Basilica of St. Francis.

Lord, teach me to rise above whatever it is that is pulling me down, preventing me from flying. I want to overcome my fears, to soar in the pure sky of your freedom. I want to be a child of light, a charioteer of the sun. Illumine my soul.

* Cf. Eloi Leclerc, *The Canticle of the Creatures: Symbols of Union* (Chicago: Franciscan Herald Press, 1970).

A Franciscan Mantle

INCE Blessed Francis was always giving away his mantle, many stories arose about this particular gesture of his, forming a little cycle of mantle stories, of which are these two; one I heard and the other I witnessed.

Once at Collestrada, near Perugia, Francis met a poor man whom he had known earlier in his life.

"How is it going with you, brother?" he asked.

But the man answered that he was in a bad way, and it was all the fault of his lord, a greedy ruler, who had taken from him practically everything he owned. He then began to curse this lord and vow that he would never forgive what the man had done to him and his family.

But Francis replied, "Dear friend, you must try to forgive your lord. Otherwise you may lose something more precious than your possessions. You may well lose your immortal soul."

"So be it, then," the man replied. "Never will I forgive that beast until he returns what he's taken." And he began again to swear, heaping curses upon his lord.

Then, without saying anything further, Francis took off his mantle and put it over the man's shoulders, indicating by his embrace that the mantle now belonged to the poor man.

So powerful was this gesture of the saint that the man, as if the spirit of Blessed Francis had entered him, began to weep and repent of his sin and beg forgiveness for his hardness of heart.

Another time, when Francis was in Rieti for treatment of his eyes, a poor woman came there seeking the same treatment. Now, when Francis saw this poor woman, he said to his father guardian, "Brother, we have to return something to its owner."

But the guardian replied, "Let it be done, then, Father Francis, if in fact we have something like that here."

"We do indeed, brother. It is a mantle that belongs to that poor woman there. Let us give it back to her now, because she has nothing in her purse to pay for her eye treatment."

"Father Francis, the mantle is mine. I have not borrowed it from anyone. But please use it as long as you want. And when you no longer have any use for it, give it back to me."

Actually the guardian had bought the mantle earlier for Francis' need, and he knew what he was going to do with it now, so he added, "Of course, holy father, you need not keep the mantle for yourself. You may do with it whatever the Spirit suggests to you."

Then Francis, relieved and full of joy, called over to me, a layman and friend of his who happened to be there, and said, "Take this mantle and twelve loaves of bread to the poor woman who is there waiting upon the doctor and tell her that the poor man to whom she loaned it no longer needs it. He thanks her and is now returning it with this bread."

So I went off and relayed Francis' message. But the

woman, thinking she was being mocked, said, "Enough with your mantle! Leave me alone, won't you?"

I insisted, however, and placed the mantle into her reluctant hands. Then, as she held the mantle, she suddenly realized that she was not being deceived. But she must have feared that what she had received so freely and easily might be taken away, for that very night she got out of bed and, not remaining for her treatment, returned home with the mantle. ✠

LORD, HOW LITTLE IS CHANGED by mere words, especially when people cannot hear because their hunger and want is speaking louder.

The laying on of one's mantle is a symbol in Sacred Scripture of imparting one's spirit to another, as when Elijah gave his mantle to Elisha (Ez 2:9–15). Let me wrap others round with a warm mantle. Let my own spirit of love flow into others by divesting myself of that excess which really belongs to them and laying it gently upon their cold and naked shoulders.

ANOTHER TALE OF
BROTHER ELIAS

TOWARD the end, when Francis was dying in the bishop's palace in Assisi, he would sing praises to God with us brothers. Or if he was too weak to sing, he would ask us to sing for him. Now the people of Assisi and I, his vicar, were worried that some neighboring town like Perugia might come and steal away our dying saint, thus depriving us of our great treasure, the final remains of the Blessed Francis. Therefore, at my insistence, the citizens of Assisi kept an armed garrison around the bishop's palace night and day.

And one day when Francis was singing a particularly joyful hymn I said, "Father Francis, you see how much reverence the people of Assisi have for you, even guarding you from their enemies. They hold you up as their saint, but now they hear you singing day after day. Will they not wonder that you take death so lightly, that you sing, instead of pray and mourn, as is seemly? So, wouldn't it be better for us to leave this place and these worldly people who crowd your solitude and return to St. Mary of the Angels?"

But Francis replied, "Oh Brother Elias, don't you remember that two years ago at Foligno the Lord revealed to me my own death, that it would come at the end of this very illness? Well, dear brother, in that same revelation the Lord assured me that all my sins are forgiven and that I will enjoy the blessedness of Paradise. How then can I pray mournfully? To be sure, before that revelation I used to weep when I thought of death and of my sins. But since then, I have only been able to rejoice whenever I think about death. I sing always and shall continue to sing to the Lord, who has given me so great a grace as the promise of Paradise. However, I do agree we should leave this palace and return to our dear Little Portion, St. Mary of the Angels. For a poor brother should not die in a palace, even that of a bishop. So make ready to carry me to the place of our Lady Poverty, for I can no longer walk."

Thereupon, we took Francis in our arms, and with a great crowd following us, we went out of the city gates and down the hill toward the plain. ❧

THE PORTIUNCULA WAS THE DEAREST place on earth to Francis, for it was the cradle of the Order. There his Order was symbolized, for St. Mary of the Angels was small and poor and under the protection of Mary, Jesus' own mother. The Portiuncula was home and hearth for Francis; it was there he would die as Christ had lived and died, in poverty, surrounded by love, in the presence of his Mother.

We wait a lifetime for the Messiah, the one the prophets promised would be coming. And when you come, Lord, you are a man walking toward us on the dusty road, a man walking with us toward food and bed, then walking ahead, your footsteps alone stronger than home in their pull upon the heart of our following.

Blessed is Mary's womb. Blessed its fruit, Jesus, our true and eternal home.

TRANSITUS

HE night that Francis died, he asked that he be placed naked upon the ground so he could wrestle naked with a naked enemy. Then, placing his hand over the wound of Christ in his side, as if to preserve the uniqueness of his own way, he said to his brothers, "I have done what was mine to do. May the Lord show you what is yours."

Because I was his Father Guardian and understood his total commitment to Lady Poverty, I went and brought a habit and undergarment and a little cap and said to him, "I am lending you these garments, Father Francis, to cover your nakedness. In holy obedience I bid you put them on, and I forbid you to give them away, for they do not belong to you."

And Francis rejoiced in the Lord that in this way he was made obedient to Lady Poverty, even to the end. Then, putting on the clothes of obedience and poverty and the little cap to cover the wounds made by the cauterizing of his eyes, he asked us brothers to praise God always and to be faithful in all ways to the Gospel of our Lord Jesus Christ.

Then he began to praise God for all things and sang over and over again "The Canticle of the Creatures," which he had composed two years before, adding a stanza to it welcoming his Sister Death and praising the Lord:

Praise to you, my Lord, for our Sister bodily death,
From whom no living person may escape.
How dreadful for those who die in sin,
How lovely for those who are found in your most holy will,
For the second death can do them no harm.

Then he began to sing Psalm 142 and raised his arms as if to welcome the embrace of his Savior. As he died, the brothers finished the psalm for him amidst joy and depths of loss untold, his body turning from its usual dark color to a gleaming white, the last words of the psalm lingering in the air, "The upright gather around me because of your generosity to me." And with his passing, one of the brothers present saw Francis borne aloft on a cloud like a giant star. ❧

BECAUSE OF ALL THE STATUES and romanticized images we have of St. Francis, it is hard for us to imagine how utterly wasted and broken this little man was when he died. Only forty-five years old, he was racked by illnesses and hemorrhaging and malnutrition brought on by extreme fasting and penance. And yet, that miserable little body was suffused with light and even broke into song! What mystery is here. It has much to do with true joy and more with true love.

St. Francis Dictates
His Testament

HE Blessed St. Francis left behind many words, including two Rules, letters, prayers, admonitions, blessings, canticles, and a testament that we brothers were to keep as his final words and his will for us for all time. And we are to treasure this testament and read it, as St. Francis instructed us, whenever we read the Rule. For his testament expresses how he wanted us to live our everyday lives. And this is what he dictated to me, his scribe, Brother Leo:

This is the way the Lord granted me, Brother Francis, to begin to do penance. When I was in sin, it seemed so bitter a thing even to look at lepers, and then the Lord himself led me among them, and I practiced mercy with them. And when I left them, that which had before seemed bitter was now changed into sweetness of soul and body. Thereupon, I lingered yet a while, and then I left the world.

And the Lord gave me such faith in churches that when I prayed there, I would pray by saying simply "We adore you, Lord Jesus Christ, here and in all your churches in the whole world, and we bless you, because by your holy cross, you have redeemed the world."

Also, the Lord gave me then, and continues to give me, such faith in priests who live in authentic communion with the Roman Catholic Church that because of their priesthood I would have recourse to them even if they persecuted me.

And if I had as great a wisdom as Solomon and I came upon poor priests of this world, I would not want to preach in their parishes if they did not want me to.

And these and all others I wish to fear, love, and honor as my lords, and I do not want to even think of their being in sin, because in them I see the Son of God and they are my lords. And I do this because with my bodily eyes I see nothing of the Most High Son of God in this world, except his most holy Body and Blood, which they alone consecrate and they alone minister to others.

And these same most holy mysteries I wish to be honored and venerated above every other thing, and I wish them kept in precious places.

And wherever I find his most holy names and his written words in unbecoming places, I want to gather them up, and I beg that they be gathered up and placed in a becoming place.

And we should honor and respect all theologians and those who announce the Word of God as those who minister to us spirit and life.

And after the Lord gave me some brothers, no one showed me what I should do, except the Most High himself, who revealed to me that we were to live according to the precepts of the Holy Gospel. And I had this written down simply and in few words, and the Lord Pope confirmed it for me.

And those who came to receive this life gave to the poor everything that was theirs, and they were content with only one tunic, padded inside and out, if they so wished, and with a cord and breeches. And they wished to have nothing else.

And we said the Divine Office, the clerics praying like other clerics, and the lay brothers praying their Our Fathers. And we were happy to live in churches. And we were unlettered and subject to all. And I worked with my hands, and I still want to, and I want all the other brothers to work at whatever is an honest job. Those who don't know how to work, should learn how, not out of the desire for wages, but to give a good example and to keep idleness at bay. But when they receive nothing for their labor, they are to have recourse to the table of the Lord, begging alms from door to door.

The Lord revealed to me that I was to greet others with, "The Lord give you peace."

The brothers are to guard rigorously against accepting churches, poor dwellings, and whatever else might be constructed for them unless they are in keeping with that Holy Poverty which we have promised in the Rule, and they can live there like "pilgrims and strangers" [1 Pt 2:11].

I firmly command as an obedience to all the brothers

that wherever they are, they do not send letters of petition to the Roman Curia either directly or through another person, neither on behalf of churches, nor other places, neither on behalf of their preaching nor because they are being persecuted. Rather, wherever they are not received, let them flee into another land to do penance with the blessing of God.

And I firmly want to obey the minister general of this brotherhood and whatever guardian he wishes to give me. And I wish to be like a slave in his hands, so that I cannot go anywhere or do anything outside of obedience and apart from his will, because he is my lord. And even though I am simple and infirm, I want always to have a cleric recite the Divine Office with me, as is written in the Rule.

And all the other brothers are bound to be obedient to their guardian and to recite the office according to the Rule. And if brothers are found not reciting the office according to the Rule, but wish to vary it somehow, or if they are not Catholics, all such brothers, wherever they are, are to be bound under the vow of obedience (and this holds even if there is only one such brother), and be sent to the custos nearest the place where they were found. And the custos is to bind them firmly to their vow of obedience, guarding them closely night and day, like men in prison, so that they cannot escape from his hands until he can personally hand them over to their minister. And the minister is firmly bound by obedience to provide an escort of brothers who will guard over them night and day, like prisoners, until they hand them over to the Lord Cardinal of Ostia, the protector and corrector of the whole brotherhood.

And let not the brothers say this is another Rule. For this is a memoir, an admonition and exhortation, and my testament, which I, Brother Francis, a poor little man, make for you, my blessed brothers, so that you might observe in a more Catholic manner the Rule we have promised the Lord.

And the minister general and all the other ministers and the custodes are bound by obedience not to add to, or remove, any of these words.

And they are always to have this writing with them, together with the Rule. And in all the chapters they hold, when they read the Rule, they are to read these words also. And I firmly command in obedience all my brothers, clerical or lay, that they do not attach explanations to the Rule and these words, saying "This is how they are to be understood." But as the Lord granted me to say and write the Rule and these words purely and simply, thus simply and without commentary are they to be understood and observed in holiness to the end.

And whoever observes these things, may he receive in Heaven the blessing of the Most High Father and on earth may he be filled with the blessing of his Beloved Son, together with the Most Holy Spirit, the Paraclete, and all the powers of heaven and all the saints. And I, Brother Francis, the least of the brothers, and your servant, as far as I am able, confirm within and without this most holy blessing. Amen. ❧

ST. FRANCIS' LAST TESTAMENT is an extraordinary document, not only in what it says, but also in what it does not say. St. Francis leaves out, for example, the incident of the Lord speaking to him from the crucifix of San Damiano, saying, "Francis, go and repair my house which, as you see, is falling into ruins," which is certainly a central event in his life. And instead St. Francis begins his Testament with his life among the lepers, as if to say, "There is where you can trust God really is: among the rejected and despised, rather than in visions and voices."

Lord, help me to remember that it is in true charity that we find you, rather than in signs and wonders. And so with St. Paul I believe that "these remain: faith, hope and love, the three of them; and the greatest of them is love" (1 Cor 13:13).

A Nun's Tale

THE Blessed Lady Clare lived on at San Damiano for twenty-seven years after the death of our Father Francis. Our community of Poor Ladies flourished, but because our convent was outside the city walls, we lived in constant danger. There were bands of mercenaries in the service of the Emperor Frederick, and Saracen archers as well, and they roamed the countryside at will destroying castles and looting cities.

In September of 1240 they came against Assisi. The Saracen archers broke through the outer wall of San Damiano and entered the cloister. Overcome with fear, we ran to take refuge around our Mother Clare, who lay ill upon a small mat on the dormitory floor.

Clare, unafraid, asked us to carry her to the cloister door and to bring along as our sole protection against the Saracens the ivory-covered silver pyx containing the Body of Christ.

Then Clare knelt before the Lord and prayed to him with many tears, saying "O Lord, behold your servants whom you have nourished with so much love. Can it be your will to hand them over to pagans? Guard them, Lord, for I am unable to take care of them now."

And from the ivory and silver ciborium, which contained the Eucharist, defender of the new covenant, came the voice of a child: "I will take care of you always."

Then the Lady Clare responded, "Lord, if it be your will, protect this city, too, for it continues to live in your love."

And the Lord Christ replied, "I will come to its aid and will protect it, but it will suffer much."

Then Clare raised her tear-filled face and comforted us. "Fear not, my daughters, for you will not be harmed. You need only have confidence in Christ."

At that very moment, realizing that they were in a holy place and in the presence of a saint protected by God, the frenzy of the Saracens turned to fear and, unnerved, they climbed down the walls even faster than they had scaled them. ✥

EACH YEAR IN ASSISI ON June 22, the people still celebrate this event in the life of their city. They call the festival Festa del Voto, and it consists of a procession of city officials, clergy, the cathedral chapter, confraternities, and citizens, to San Damiano and the Basilica of St. Clare, where they offer long wax candles to the church. For seven centuries this ceremony has been performed in gratitude to Clare for the city's deliverance, an example to us all of the importance of remembering the great events of our past.

It was the Holy Eucharist that worked the miracle of Assisi's deliverance, and one of the meanings of Eucharist is remembrance. We remember, we "do this in memory" of Christ, who asked us to do so.

Lord, as the people of Assisi remember the miracle of the deliverance of their city through the intercession of St.

Clare, let me remember the miracle you effect in every Eucharist, the transformation of bread and wine into your Body and Blood that I might be transformed.

THE GOLDEN SAYINGS OF BROTHER GILES

 BROTHER Giles, the third companion of Francis, joined the Lesser Brothers when I was only eighteen years old. I was a citizen of Assisi and was deeply imbued with the ideals of chivalry and eager for great, heroic deeds, which I'd heard the troubadours sing about, but by the mercy of God, I followed God's Troubadour, Francis, instead, and grew in prayer and the love of God. I survived Francis by more than thirty-five years and was known far and wide as a master of prayer and contemplation. Many people came to me to hear my words of life, and my words were remembered. . . .

There are three things so great and useful that if you possess them, you cannot fall into evil: in peace and for God's sake, putting up with all tribulation that may befall you; humbling yourself more and more in all you do and receive; loving faithfully those goods which cannot be seen with the eyes of the flesh.

Everything that can be thought of, seen, told, and touched, is nothing compared to what cannot be thought of, seen, told, or touched.

All of Holy Scripture speaks to us the way a mother speaks to her baby in that lisping baby talk. Otherwise we could not understand the words.

Sinners need never despair of God's mercy while they live; for there is hardly a tree so thorny and gnarled that we cannot make it smooth and pretty and ornament it. All the more, there is no sinner in the world so gnarled that God cannot smooth and adorn that person with grace and virtues.

I once said to a certain brother who was my spiritual friend, "Do you believe that I love you?" And the brother answered, "Yes, I do believe you love me." But I said to him, "Don't believe it, brother, for the Creator alone loves the creature; and the love of the creature is nothing compared to the love of the Creator."

You see how actors and jongleurs wonderfully commemorate those who give them even a piece of clothing. What then should we do for the Lord, our God?

The extent to which you are ready to bear tribulations and injuries for God's sake is the extent to which you are great before God. And the extent to which you are cowardly in bearing tribulations and sorrows for God's sake is the extent to which you are less before God and to which you do not know who God is.

It is much better to bear one grievous wrong for the love of God without any complaining than to feed a hundred poor people for many days and to fast for many days from morning until the stars come out.

If you wish to be saved, don't hope for that consolation which a mortal creature can give you, for the falls that occur from consolation are greater and more frequent than those arising from tribulation.

People ask God for gifts without measure and without end, but they wish to serve him with measure and with end.

The more you are in a state of grace, the more you are attacked by the Devil. But this should not deter you from living on in grace, for the harder the fight, the greater will be the crown if you prevail.

To contemplate is to be separated from all and to be united with God alone.

I do not consider it a lesser virtue to know how to keep silence well than to know how to speak well. In fact, it seems to me that we should all have necks like cranes so that our speech would have to pass through many joints before leaving our mouth.

If you were to live a thousand years and not have anything to do outside yourself, you would have enough to do inside, in your own heart. ❦

IN THESE "GOLDEN SAYINGS," we see far more than pious platitudes. Here is Giles: his very self is revealed in these sayings. His personality speaks in answer to questions we all have had, even today, almost eight hundred years later. Giles understood poverty, he understood Francis, the Little Poor One, and he understood the Franciscan message, as his words reveal. They echo in simplicity and redoubtable truth. We hear no hesitation, no subjugation, as if his conversations came straight from experience—from one who "had been there" from the beginning to the end.

Lord, let me remember that every word I speak reflects my experience of you. Teach me the words that live.

THE ROBBER'S TALE

ITH the deep forest and isolated highways of my times, being a robber was an easy and rewarding profession. Yet, once at Monte Casale two friends and I came upon Francis of Assisi—a poor traveler who gave us nothing for our efforts in robbing him but a story about the glory of poverty and the riches of heaven.

But so impressed were we with the holiness and manner of life of this Francis that all three of us left the world and entered a friary on the same mountain. Shortly thereafter, my two other companions died in the Lord, but I lived on, in penance and mourning for my sins and in praise of him who would one day receive me with love and glory. For fifteen years I fasted on bread and water three days a week and was content with only one garment. I always went about barefoot, and I never slept after praying matins at midnight.

After many years, when Francis himself had gone to Heaven, I was trying to pray matins and discovered I no longer had the strength to continue. I was so weary that I fell upon my bed and slept.

As soon as my head hit the pillow, I was lifted up to a high mountain precipice below which were jagged rocks and rough cliffs jutting out in every direction. Then the one guiding me pushed me off the precipice, and I plummeted headlong over the rocks. I fell from ledge to ledge, hitting one boulder after another until I came to rest at the foot of the mountain. All my limbs felt shattered and my bones fractured, but I was still conscious, so that I could hear my guide saying "Get up now, there's still a long way to go."

But I replied, "What a cruel and unreasonable man you are! Here I am, shattered almost to death, and you bid me get up?"

Then the guide came up to me and touched me and my limbs were instantly healed.

Next he took me and showed me a vast plain covered with sharp rocks, thorns, briar bushes, and muddy swamps.

"Now brother, you must walk barefoot across this plain and enter the fiery furnace that you can see flaming at the other end."

And so I did as the angel commanded and succeeded in crossing the plain, not without great agony. And when I reached the furnace, the angel said, "Now you must go into the furnace!"

"Ah me," I replied. "What a heartless guide you are! After that agonizing passage across the plain, you bid me enter this furnace, without so much as a brief rest?"

But as I spoke, I saw devils standing all around me. Then suddenly, without warning, they lifted their red-hot pitchforks and thrust me into the furnace. But the angel let me stand amid the flames only briefly before pulling me out and saying "Prepare now to move on to the danger you still have to face."

"O cruel guide," I answered, "you have no compassion

at all. Here I am almost consumed by fire and you lead me on to further danger."

But the angel touched me again, and my burns were completely healed.

Then he led me to a bridge I could not cross without the greatest difficulty, for it was narrow and slippery, and flowing beneath it was a wild river full of serpents, reptiles, scorpions, and toads, and it emitted a horrible stench.

"Now you must cross that bridge," said the angel.

"But how can I without falling in?"

"Follow after me and put your foot exactly where I put mine, and you will cross the bridge in safety."

And so I followed in the footsteps of the angel until, in the middle of the bridge, the angel left me and flew up to a magnificent building set on a very high hill. I watched the angel fly away and realized I was all alone in the middle of the bridge with all those ugly river creatures raising their heads out of the water, ready to devour me if I fell.

I could neither go forward nor backward, so I stood paralyzed with fear, not knowing what to do. In desperation I bent down and embraced the bridge; knowing in my heart that there was no help save in God, I began to call upon the Lord Jesus Christ to help me in his holy and righteous mercy. And as I prayed I seemed to be growing wings. I began to rejoice and watch the wings grow, hoping to fly up to the place where the angel had flown. But I was too eager and tried to fly before the wings were fully grown. Thus, my wings failed in flight and I crashed down upon the bridge, and all the feathers dropped from the wings.

Terrified and clinging to the bridge, I again called upon

the mercy of Christ. Again I felt the wings sprouting, but as before, I tried to fly before the wings were fully grown and fell headlong onto the bridge a second time, the feathers once again falling out.

Realizing at last that it was my haste that had twice prevented me from flying, I said to myself, "If I begin to sprout wings a third time, I will wait until I am ready to fly."

I decided to wait and pray, and it seemed like a century and a half before the third sprouting of wings. But this time I waited until I was certain the wings were fully grown. Then I flew boldly up to the building on the hill, where the angel had flown. But when I reached the door of that lovely dwelling, the doorkeeper said, "Who are you to come here?"

"I am a Lesser Brother," I replied.

"Then wait until I summon St. Francis and see if he recognizes you."

While I was waiting, I looked at the walls of that wondrous city and saw that they were transparent, so that I could see clearly the wonderful choir of saints and everything else that was happening inside. Then out came St. Francis and Brother Bernard and Brother Giles and, behind St. Francis, a multitude of saintly men and women beyond numbering.

Then St. Francis said to the doorkeeper, "Let him in, for he is indeed one of my brothers."

And he took me in and showed me things wonderful to behold. And I instantly felt such sweetness and consolation that I forgot all the sufferings I had undergone, even as if I had never been in the world below.

But St. Francis said to me, "Son, now you must return to the world for seven days to prepare yourself as you will. Then I will come for you and bring you to this wonderful place of the blessed."

St. Francis wore a star-studded stole and his five stigmata gleamed like stars so bright that they seemed to illumine the whole city. And Brother Bernard wore a most beautiful crown of stars. Brother Giles was completely robed in light, and I recognized many other Lesser Brothers with St. Francis, and others, too, I had never seen before.

Then, reluctantly taking my leave, I returned to the world just as the brothers were ringing the bell for prime. No more time had elapsed than that between matins and prime, though it had seemed like many years.

I related my vision to the guardian of Monte Casale, and within seven days I fell into a fever. On the seventh day St. Francis came with a shining company of saints and led me to the place of the blessed. ❧

IN THIS STORY IT IS CLEAR that the brother is being shown in a dream the great trials he has already endured. In images that are reminiscent of the Quest of the Holy Grail, he sees himself overcoming one obstacle after another because it is the Lord's angel himself who is leading him.

Lord Jesus, I, too, have known obstacles I thought I could not overcome, and then you have enabled me to do so, often by means of guides I thought were cruel at the time, because they led me where my cowardice or laziness did not want to go.

And if I could see my whole life in a dream, as this brother does, I pray that I, too, would see my life as a quest leading to you. I pray that everything I've suffered and everything I've overcome would be revealed as necessary, in order to come to you. For you, Lord Jesus, are the reward of all our trials, the end of all our seeking.

AFTERWORD

IT CAME TO ME SUDDENLY, as most insights do
when you've been thinking about something for a long
time, trying to see the whole picture. Picture. Image. That
was it. I had been trying to picture Francis of Assisi in his
milieu, and then suddenly one Sunday morning, as I was
reading the *New York Times Magazine* over a cup of coffee,
an image of Francis came into my imagination, and I realized that Francis himself is the image of the idea I was
trying to formulate about him. He stood there in my imagination, an icon of the Gospel life in an age that had lost a
clear image of what the Gospel life is. I saw clearly that it is
not so much his writings, his Rule and teachings, but Francis himself who is the icon of Christ. Francis himself as he
is painted in the early Franciscan tales. The countenance of
his radical poverty, chastity, and obedience became in my
mind's eye an emerging Polaroid print, growing clearer of
itself, without my having anything to do about it.

The image of a Polaroid print made me think of conven-
tional photography and I saw Christianity at the time of St.
Francis as a black-and-white negative you have to hold up
to the sun to see, and then only in reversed images. The
poor, chaste, obedient Christ had faded into his very negative, especially as exhibited in corrupt clergy and religious,
whose greed, lechery, and self-will reversed the image of
Christ. People no longer recognized Christ in many of the
official representatives of the Church. And since there were

few books, and those that existed were painstakingly copied and jealously guarded by literate monks and their patrons, for whose eyes alone the exquisite illuminations shone, God sent Francis to become a developed negative, an illuminated icon of the person transformed into Jesus Christ.

Then another image flashed across my mind's screen: the cartoon and the finished fresco. The artists of the time would make sketches of their proposed frescoes, and these sketches were called cartoons. The image I have of the medieval Church immediately before Francis is that of a fresco that has faded back into the bare outlines of its own cartoon, and there is no one to bring back the freshness and color of the original image.

Then along comes Francis of Assisi and his followers, and the fresco begins to take on color and life and move through the countryside like a fluid painting. And it is authentic to everyone who views it, because it restores precisely what has faded out in the original: the features of the icon of the Father, Jesus Christ.

Francis, icon of the Savior. Francis and his followers, frescoes of the true Church. It is not what Francis did in the Church, then, that is so important, but the image that Francis and his followers became. They imaged what the Church and each individual Christian can be. He held up an icon that people recognized as a mirror both of Christ and of themselves, provided they were indeed what they were meant to be. And the more Francis lived the Gospel literally and radically, the clearer the picture became.

And that is the secret of the tales of Francis of Assisi.

They show us a living, moving, breathing image of Jesus Christ, and that alone draws people to God. No amount of teaching and preaching, of directives and censures, of encyclical letters of reform like those of the Popes of his time or ours, can substitute for a human being become Christ to his or her age.

That image begins to be duplicated, not only in lives, but in stone and paint and words, in music and dress and manners. And a fresh, contemporary image of Christianity begins to emerge like a Polaroid print that has remained obscure and undeveloped and then by some marvelous alchemy begins to develop into a clear picture. Francis of Assisi was God's alchemist of the thirteenth century. And his life was the catalyst that transformed a negative image, a faded fresco, into living color.

A Chronology of the Life of St. Francis

1182   Francis is born in Assisi; he is baptized John, but his father, returning from a trip to France, nicknames him Francesco ("Frenchman").

1193   Clare is born in Assisi to Favarone and Ortolana of the House of Offreduccio.

1198   The citizens of Assisi destroy the Rocca Maggiore, the fortress that towered above the city, a symbol of the Emperor's presence.

1199–1200   Civil war in Assisi results in the establishment of the commune.

1202 (November)   War between Assisi and Perugia. At the battle of Ponte San Giovanni, a town midway between the two warring towns, Francis is captured and taken as a prisoner to Perugia for one year.

1203–04   Francis is freed and returns to Assisi. He is ill during the whole of the year 1204.

1205 (Spring)   Francis decides to join the Papal Army in Apulia, south of Rome, which is under the command of Walter of Brienne. He leaves home and journeys only as far as neighboring Spoleto, where he is told in a dream to return to Assisi.

1205 (Summer)   The final summer with his friends as "King of the Youth of Assisi."

1205 (Fall)   San Damiano crucifix instructs Francis, "Go and repair my house, which, as you see, is falling into ruin." Francis takes some of his father's cloth to Foligno and sells it. He gives the money to the priest of San Damiano, who refuses it. Beginning of conflict with his father.

1206 (Spring)   Francis' father takes him before the civil court for the return of his money. When Francis says he is no longer subject to the civil authorities because he is consecrated to God, his father takes him before Bishop Guido. There Francis renounces his patrimony in front of the bishop and assembled citizens and then leaves for Gubbio, where he nurses the lepers.

1206 (Summer)   Francis returns to Assisi dressed as a hermit and begins to repair San Damiano.

1206 (Summer)–1208 (February)   Francis repairs San Damiano, the small chapel of St. Peter (which is no longer standing), and the Portiuncula (St. Mary of the Angels).

1208 (February 24)   At the Portiuncula, Francis hears the Gospel for the Feast of St. Matthias and embraces Gospel poverty. He changes his leather belt for a rope cincture. He begins to preach.

1208 (April 16)   Bernard of Quintavalle and Peter Catanii join Francis.

1208 (April 23)   Giles of Assisi joins them.

1208 (Summer)   Three new members join.

1208 (late)   The seven brothers go to Poggio Bustone and preach throughout the Rieti Valley. A new brother joins.

1209 (early)   The eight return to the Portiuncula. Four more join them.

1209 (Spring)   Francis writes a short Rule and leaves for Rome with his first eleven brothers. Pope Innocent III approves their way of life. They return and settle at Rivo Torto, on the plain below Assisi.

1210   A peasant and his donkey invade their shed at Rivo Torto, and the brothers leave and go to the Portiuncula.

1211   Francis plans to go to Syria, but high winds ruin his plans.

1212 (March 18–19)   On the night after Palm Sunday, Francis receives Clare and her cousin Pacifica into the Order at the Portiuncula and locates them first at two Benedictine convents before Bishop Guido, several weeks later, gives the church of San Damiano as a home to Clare and her companions (including her sister Agnes, who has since joined them).

1215 (November)   Francis, in Rome for the Fourth Lateran Council, meets St. Dominic.

1216 (July 16)   Pope Innocent III dies in Perugia. Two days later Honorius III is chosen to replace him.

1216 (Summer)   In Perugia, Francis obtains from Pope Honorius the Plenary Indulgence (sometimes called the Portiuncula Pardon) to commemorate the consecration of the Portiuncula.

1217 (May 5)   At the General Chapter at the Portiuncula, the first missionary brothers are sent forth to cross the Alps and the Mediterranean.

1219 (late June)   Francis leaves Ancona for Acre in Syria, where he stays only a few days before setting out for Damietta in Egypt.

1219 (Autumn)   Francis meets the Sultan in Damietta and later visits the Holy Land.

1220   Francis returns to Italy and resigns as minister general. He chooses Peter Catanii to replace him.

1221 (March 10)   Peter Catanii dies. Elias is designated vicar general.

1221 (May 30)   General Chapter and First Rule.

1223   At Fonte Colombo, Francis composes the Second Rule, to be discussed in the General Chapter in June. Pope Honorius III approves it on November 29.

1223 (December 24–25)   Christmas at Greccio. Beginning of the custom of the Christmas crib.

1224 (August 15–September 29)   Francis goes to La Verna to prepare for the Feast of St. Michael, September 29. On September 14 or 15 he receives the stigmata.

1224 (October and early November) Francis returns to the Portiuncula.

1224–1225 (December to February) Riding a donkey, Francis undertakes a preaching tour through Umbria and the Marches.

1225 (March–May) His eyesight worsens; nearly blind, he spends some time at San Damiano. He composes the "Canticle of the Creatures."

1225 Adds the verse to the "Canticle" on Pardon and Peace and a reconciliation takes place between the bishop and the mayor of Assisi. Francis leaves for Rieti.

1225 Francis is welcomed in Rieti by his friend Cardinal Ugolino, the future Pope Gregory IX, who recommends his eyes be cauterized. Francis goes to Fonte Colombo for the cauterization, but it is delayed until Brother Elias arrives.

1225 (September) Another doctor treats Francis' eyes.

1226 (April) Francis is in Siena for another eye treatment.

1226 (May or June) Francis is at La Cella in Cortona, where he dictates his testament. Returns to the Portiuncula.

1226 (July and August) Because of the heat, Francis stays at Bagnara, in the mountains near Nocera.

1226 (late August or early September) His condition worsens, and he returns to Assisi, where he resides at the bishop's palace.

1226 (September) Francis senses his death is near and insists on returning to the Portiuncula.

1226 (Saturday October 3) Francis dies at the Portiuncula; he is buried the next day in San Giorgio in Assisi, where today the Basilica of St. Clare has replaced the Church of San Giorgio.

1227 Cardinal Ugolino is elected Pope Gregory IX.

1228 (July 16) Gregory IX canonizes Francis in Assisi.

1230 (May 25) The body of St. Francis is transferred from San Giorgio to the new basilica constructed in his honor.

1253 (August 11) St. Clare dies at San Damiano and is buried in the Church of San Giorgio, where the body of Francis was first buried.

1255 (August 12) Pope Alexander IV canonizes St. Clare at Anagni.

1259 Alexander IV ratifies by Papal bull the move of the Poor Ladies from San Damiano to the Church of San Giorgio, where St. Clare's body lay buried. They were already residing there, having moved shortly after the death of St. Clare. They take with them to San Giorgio the crucifix that had spoken to Francis, the silver and ivory pyx with which St. Clare had dispelled the Saracens, the iron grate through which they received Holy Communion and through which they had viewed the body of St. Francis for the last time. The Poor Ladies remain at San Giorgio, which is eventually replaced by the Basilica of St. Clare, where the Poor Ladies reside today.

ACKNOWLEDGMENTS

I gratefully acknowledge the long hours of editing and the many suggestions and rewordings of Susan Saint Sing; the encouragement and patience of Patricia Kossmann, my editor at Doubleday; and the scholarship of Fr. Théophile Desbonnets, O.F.M., whose book *Assise sur les pas de saint François,* was invaluable in framing the chronology and in the selection of stories relating to the places of St. Francis' life.

I would also like to acknowledge and thank my Provincial, Fr. Jeremy Harrington, O.F.M., and all the brothers I live with for their support and encouragement.

MURRAY BODO is a Franciscan priest. He is writer-in-residence at Thomas More College, Crestview Hills, Kentucky, where he teaches composition and creative writing. Father Murray is the author of numerous books on Franciscan subjects, including *Francis: The Journey and the Dream* and *Clare, A Light in the Garden.*